In the Wake of Waco

from the Library of Kenneth Slawson
Mary

26 July '99

In the Wake of Waco

Why Were Adventists Among the Victims?

Cari Hoyt Haus and Madlyn Lewis Hamblin

Review and Herald® Publishing Association
Hagerstown, MD 21740

The authors assume full responsibility for the accuracy of all facts and quotations as cited in this book.

This book was
Edited by Richard W. Coffen and Gerald Wheeler
Designed by Bill Kirstein
Cover design by Helcio Deslandes
Cover photo by AP/Wide World Photos
Typeset: 11.5 Clearface

PRINTED IN U.S.A.

98 97 96 95 94 93 10 9 8 7 6 5 4 3 2 1

R&H Cataloging Service
Haus, Cari Hoyt
In the wake of Waco: why were Adventists among the victims? by Cari Hoyt Haus and Madlyn Lewis Hamblin.

1. Koresh, David. 2. Branch Davidians. 3. Waco, Texas. Mount Carmel. I. Hamblin, Madlyn Lewis, joint author. II. Title.

291.9

ISBN 0-8280-0813-2

DEDICATION

Dedicated to

all the victims of Waco

CONTENTS

	Preface	9
Chapter 1	Set for a Showdown	11
Chapter 2	Horror at the Compound	18
Chapter 3	Sifting Through the Ashes	27
Chapter 4	Always Looking for Something	37
Chapter 5	Motor City Madman	45
Chapter 6	Six-shooter Junction	55
Chapter 7	Roller-coaster Religion	64
Chapter 8	Preparation of a People	72
Chapter 9	The Seductive Seven Seals	80
Chapter 10	Little Women in Waiting	92
Chapter 11	The Australian Connection	99
Chapter 12	Honolulu Gold Mine	105
Chapter 13	Nixed at Newbold?	111
Chapter 14	The Bucks Behind the Behavior	117
Chapter 15	Sinner Without Equal	123
Chapter 16	The Enforcers	130
Chapter 17	How Unlucky Can You Get?	136
Chapter 18	Why Adventists Were Vulnerable	141
Chapter 19	The Mind Behind the Mania	159
Chapter 20	It Has Happened Before	168
Chapter 21	It Will Happen Again	178
Chapter 22	Those Magnetic Mass Movements	183
Chapter 23	Steps and Stages of Faith	203
Chapter 24	Escaping the Extremes	216
	Epilogue	223

PREFACE

For 51 days the world watched with fascination as a group of Branch Davidians, imprisoning themselves in their fortress-like compound, defied a group of federal agents.

It all began on February 28, 1993, with the worst loss of life among federal law enforcement personnel in this century. Four Bureau of Alcohol, Tobacco, and Firearms agents died in a shoot-out with the followers of self-proclaimed prophet David Koresh.

On the fifty-first day of the lengthy standoff, my husband came home for lunch and flicked on the TV. "Something's happening in Waco," he said.

It was April 19, 1993, a day I will never forget. Along with millions of other Americans, I sat riveted to the screen as satellites beamed the now-familiar picture of a barricaded compound into my living room. All morning tanks had rammed the 50-room complex, pumping in torrents of tear gas.

Before my horrified eyes and millions of others, wisps of smoke began to curl from the compound. Within the next 45 minutes, Ranch Apocalypse, home to both my high school home economics teacher (Sherri Jewell) and church school friend (Jeff Little), ignited into a full-blown inferno and burned to the ground.

That night I couldn't sleep. I felt an overwhelming sadness. Why had these friends from my high school years chosen to follow cult leader David Koresh to the death? What had attracted them to this man, anyway? And what could I do—if anything—to secure the future safety of my own children from such a fate?

After all, even though the Seventh-day Adventist Church claimed no connection to the fiery fiasco or to the Davidians, the fact remained that a large percentage of those inside were former Seventh-day Adventists. Some may have still had their names on the church books. My two friends, Sherri and Jeff, were likable, kind, and intelligent human beings. The questions rolled continuously through my mind. Why were so many ex-Adventists in the compound? Did they stay of their own accord, or were they trapped in the end? How did Koresh get them to believe his bizarre doctrines? And what made Seventh-day Adventists vulnerable to the likes of David Koresh?

My mind continued to whirl. Answering all these questions wouldn't be easy. Yet I felt a burning desire to find out "why."

As I often do when troubled, I rose at 5:00 a.m. and put my thoughts on paper. Those thoughts later became an article. Yet I still had questions—many more.

• Why did intelligent, educated people give up their incomes, wives, freedom, and lives for a mentally unbalanced high school dropout?

• How could Koresh's followers possibly have believed that he was the "Messiah"?

• What *did* Koresh teach?

• Why did the ATF believe it was necessary to storm Ranch Apocalypse?

• What could we as a nation and as individuals have done to prevent this debacle?

• Are there things we can do now to make sure another Waco doesn't happen? Or is another inferno inevitable?

Many Seventh-day Adventists are asking the same questions.

In writing this book, Madlyn and I must credit Penny Estes Wheeler for her encouragement and invaluable help. Also a big thank you goes to Gary Patterson, administrative assistant to the president of the North American Division, for assistance in obtaining documented stories and interviews. Special appreciation is extended to our husbands, David and Ray, for their patient support. Finally, our deep desire is that this information will strengthen your faith in God's inspired Word and motivate you to search it for yourself, uncovering the truths it contains.

Cari Haus

Chapter One

Set for a Showdown

The shades of a spectacular sunset filled the clear night sky over Waco, Texas. Thousands of glorious wildflowers bloomed with deceptive beauty in the surrounding fields as the impending darkness settled over the nubby landscape. An ominous chill enveloped the area, bringing with it a steady, drizzling rain.

As the night deepened, so did the anxiety of hundreds of well-armed federal agents camped 10 miles from Waco. For 51 days they'd been guarding a sprawling, city-block-sized fortress on 77 dusty acres. Tacked together with tar paper and covered with beige clapboard siding, the ragtag jumble of bullet-pocked buildings literally groaned with used lumber. The large slapdash wooden structure contained 50 rooms and about twice that many stubborn residents. But despite its poor construction, the complex of interlocking buildings offered some degree of safety from the overwhelming firepower arrayed against it.

A shift of FBI snipers nestled uncomfortably into bullet-pocked hideouts fronted with sandbags. Their weary eyes stared across a no-man's-land into the sentry tower and spotlighted windows of the compound.

On the horizon, a rusting hulk of a watertower loomed above the shaky fortress, while a tattered Star of David flag whipped in the steady wind. And inside the ugly four-story watchtower, six Branch Davidian sentries, trying to detect any FBI movement, squinted into the blinding stadium-style searchlights. Dressed in black pajamalike fighting outfits and ski masks, they peered through fortified firing ports.

◆◆◆

Well prepared for the standoff, the Davidians had stockpiled nearly $200,000 worth of firepower. Their deadly stash included semiautomatic rifles, grenades, and more than 1 million rounds of ammunition. The pantry held a hoard of literally thousands of military-style "meals ready to eat." During the past year Davidian women had purchased hundreds of pounds of beans and other staples and had prepared shelf after shelf of carefully canned food. With their lethal wealth of weapons, ammunition, and enough food to last for one to two years, the persistent cult members were in no hurry to cave in and end the siege.

The standoff had begun with a bloody 45-minute shoot-out on February 28, 1993, when federal agents stormed the fortified compound. As a result, four federal agents and six cult members died. Additional numbers had suffered injuries. The attack turned out to be one of the worst fiascos in federal law enforcement history.

That's when hundreds of federal agents and county lawmen—all waiting for signs of surrender—had surrounded the shoddy ranch buildings.

◆◆◆

Now, on this eerie night 51 days after the fatal shoot-out, the captive cult showed signs of stress but not capitulation. In the meantime, irritation and fatigue fueled a growing impatience among the FBI agents. Negotiations with the cult had hit increasingly turbulent waters. And the estimated $500,000 per week required to maintain the siege drew flak from politicians and the public alike.

Voluntary surrender seemed unlikely. David Koresh, the cult leader, had continually irritated the FBI with harangues about the Bible and demands for time. He also had requested word-processing equipment so that he could write his prophetic interpretation of the seven seals of Revelation 6.

Although Koresh was far from finished with his book about the seven seals, the FBI was finished with him. Federal agents had grown totally intolerant of his frequent lies and broken promises.

More than anything else, they desired a nonviolent and quick solution—one that gave priority to the safety of the more than 17 children thought to be trapped inside the compound walls. And the FBI wanted David Koresh brought to justice for the murder of their luckless ATF colleagues.

Razor wire, sharp enough to make human flesh look like ground hamburger, ringed the compound. Psychological warfare between the two sides had already raged as fiercely as any physical battle. The FBI had continually blasted Koresh and his followers with a barrage of earsplitting, irritating noise. FBI "selections" ranged from the squeals of rabbits being slaughtered to the constant high-pitched whine of a dentist's drill. A once-popular and now timely song, "These Boots Were Made for Walkin'," ranked high on the "FBI Top 40."

Cult members responded to the blasted bombardment by wearing earplugs. In retaliation, Koresh reached into his own arsenal of sound. He and his band staged their own mini-rock concerts, and they weren't of the Muzak office music variety! Children and adults alike endured the nerve-shattering noise exploding from the compound, inflicted on them as though broadcast from a hellish radio station. The round-the-clock performances by off-the-hook phones, chanting Tibetan monks, Christmas crooners, and military cadets again and again broadsided the compound and ears of those inside.

In this war of nerves cult members ate, slept, and wondered about their future.

In addition to the "music," agents surrounding the compound "generously provided" the cult with all-night lighting. Blinding spotlights glared angrily into the windows, making it difficult for the Davidians to sleep.

Inside the 50-room fortress waited 5-year-old Star and 9-year-old Cyrus Koresh. Said to be Koresh's favorite children, they were a bright-eyed and spunky twosome. But they must have slept uneasily in their lighted sleeping quarters. During the 51-day siege Star and Cyrus had met death face-to-face, even witnessing a full-scale gun battle. But through it all they still played innocently among the trash now littering the floors. Taught to expect the showdown, they had quickly grown accustomed to the bullet-stopping bales of hay stacked inside the front walls of the compound. And the reinforced firing ports, ringing the walls as a safe haven for the "Mighty Men" of the cult, must have fascinated them.

On that last wet night an alert FBI sniper kept the cult's constantly patrolling sentries in his sights. Suddenly he noticed something unusual above the spotlighted compound. "Wait a minute," he said as he motioned to a fellow sharpshooter. From within the compound an SOS flashed into the sky.

Mounting tension inside the compound had forced someone into action, although the floodlights must have blinded him or her to agent movements all around.

The Morse code signals continued. "SOS . . . FBI negotiations have broken down. We want the press."

The FBI agents huddled in the drizzling rain and waited tensely for the morning . . . and for what they hoped would be a final resolution to the showdown.

◆◆◆

In Galesburg, Michigan, Pat and Lonnie Little slept only uneasily. Their 31-year-old son, Jeff, remained in the compound. Attempts to reach him had proven unsuccessful.

Back in Waco FBI officers had already gone door-to-door to houses near the compound, telling people to stay inside. "There might be some noise," one officer had warned. Officials advised several residents to visit relatives for the day.

At just 57 minutes until dawn, the FBI made its first move. The showdown began with a phone call. Steve Schneider, Koresh's top lieutenant, picked up the phone.

"In a few minutes we're going to gas the compound," Steve heard an urgent voice say. "This is not an assault," the voice continued. "Please instruct everyone to exit from your buildings and surrender."

Furious, Schneider ripped the special phone from the wall, stormed to a window, and flung the phone into the yard. In so doing, he completely isolated himself and more than 75 men, women, and children inside the tinderbox walls of the cult's headquarters.

Outside the compound, grim-faced troopers climbed into their drab green tanks, pulled back the throttles, and lumbered toward the dilapidated string of buildings.

Cult members, peering from their windows, saw them coming. For some unexplainable reason, someone held a small child up to the window as sporadic bursts of gunfire spit at the oncoming armada of vehicles. Unarmed but heavily armored, the approaching tanks did not fire back.

If anyone was still sleeping during the opening of the drama, it couldn't have been for long, because the barrage of noise was about to begin again, only this time it wasn't "music."

◆◆◆

David Koresh, positioned in his secluded room on the fourth floor of the watchtower, called his top lieutenants to join in his final stand. The men in black emerged from their assigned quarters, which were separate from those occupied by the women and children.

Compound residents, trapped by their fierce commitment and unbridled devotion to Koresh, understood the danger of any escape because of, in part, the razor wire—those murderous coils of steel able to tear human flesh to shreds. Even more deadly were the sentry sharpshooters, Koresh's Mighty Men, who had rifles ready to stop in their tracks any would-be traitors that might attempt to leave the compound.

The poorly constructed wooden buildings that the cult children called home contained a large cache of unusually flammable materials. Weapons and loose hay were strewn everywhere. Truckloads of ammunition, lantern fuel, and a huge propane tank added to the combustibles.

From outside Ranch Apocalypse an FBI agent barked an order into his two-way radio. Hundreds of federal agents quickly surrounded the compound, although they kept a healthy distance. Although gunfire again erupted from the compound, the FBI agents continued to hold their fire.

On the outskirts of the compound scores of reporters and photographers tried to wake up. As tanks started to move, they felt their adrenalin start to spurt. With shaky hands the photographers removed the lens caps from their cameras and jockeyed their tripods for the best position. At last—the long-awaited action!

The FBI agents crawled forward at a snail's pace. Tired of long shifts and near-capacity hotels, they were ready for this day.

The sun peeked over the horizon, and buzzards circled overhead. A 30-mile-per-hour wind picked up while the tanks continued their steady push forward.

"Take cover!" a law enforcement man shouted to nearby journalists as gunfire once again erupted from the watchtower. Although stationed a full two miles from the compound, the media people were still within range of the cult's powerful 50-millimeter machine gun.

It was 6:00 a.m.

When Steve Schneider had disconnected that phone, he had

unwittingly said no once and for all to the FBI demand for surrender. In response the FBI launched phase two of their plan.

A 58-ton combat tank, now in position, left the others and swung toward Ranch Apocalypse. It rumbled along at its top speed of 29 miles per hour.

Its destination? The front door of the compound.

Chapter Two

Horror at the Compound

The morning dawned bright and clear in Galesburg, Michigan. As usual Pat Little kept a watchful eye on the TV screen. Because the siege involving her son Jeff had stretched into 51 days, there often was not much news from Ranch Apocalypse. But for some reason today seemed to be different. Pat picked up her phone and dialed her oldest son, Aaron. He was still asleep.

"They're having it on every few minutes," she said into his answering machine. "So there might be something happening today."

Near the compound the 58-ton tank pushed up to the locked front door. It was the same door that Koresh had closed in the ATF agents' faces 51 days earlier. The olive-drab brute lowered its hydraulic blade and then slammed it into the flimsy wall. Within minutes the 30-foot-by-12-foot metallic machine had smashed a gaping hole to the left of the door.

As the battering began, walls within the compound trembled violently. Sleeping Mighty Men, crammed four to a room, leaped from their crude wooden bunk beds. As the ramming continued, they picked up automatic weapons and scattered to safer areas.

Women in their own spartan second-floor lair and the children in an adjacent room hurriedly donned gas masks. While the tank continued to hit the building, Davidian sentries—from their firing ports in the four-story watchtower—responded to the massive intruder with some 80 rounds of gunfire. Agents operating the metallic monster continued their destructive work but did not fire back.

At the same time FBI loudspeakers blared a continual message. "This is not an assault. Do not fire! Exit the compound and follow instructions."

Within the besieged buildings not a soul moved toward the door. Moments later a long boom from the tank reached inside the hole in the front wall and shot torrents of tear gas into the building. Terrified men, women, and children sprang into action, dodging the jets of tear gas. Shreds of Sheetrock and splintered wood flew everywhere.

Outside, buses stood ready for the men, women, and children whom the FBI fully expected to emerge. But no one exited the compound.

The tear gas being pumped inside the Branch Davidian complex actually had been banned for international use by the Geneva Convention. Forced out by compressed air, the fine, yellowish, crystal powder disabled persons hit with it for as long as 10 minutes.

As the terrifying gas attack continued, an even greater mental turmoil raged in the minds of shaken cult members. But a sense of grim commitment pervaded the compound, much stronger than any desire to escape the agonizing fumes. Doomed to damnation if they ran and doomed to die if they stayed, they found themselves powerless to muster sufficient courage or independence to obey their own survival instincts. Some may have tried to escape but may have been shot, or the exits were blocked by the ramming.

Mothers shielded their young children, for whom the masks were not as effective, from the stinging yellow spray. They quickly squelched any desire to flee what they called Ranch Apocalypse. As the attacks continued, the protective gas masks became less effective. Confusion reigned as torrent after torrent of the disabling spray stung the skin, eyes, nose, and throat of anyone daring to remove his or her mask. Forced shut by the gas, cult members' eyes flooded with tears as the Davidians huddled in agony on the floor.

Through its newly created entry point the M728 tank continued to spray 15-second doses of tear gas into the compound. Gas mask filters clogged again and again. Cult members removed them briefly to blow out accumulations of the pesky powder. Wet handkerchiefs also offered some protection from the chemical onslaught. Occasionally those outside could see cult members hunkering down while the tank continued to crash into their building from all sides.

Periodically, gusting winds blew through the walls, diluting the gas. Men, women, and children alike scrambled for the fresh air. The gas, while irritating, was bearable in some areas. Cultists crouched or lay on the floor gasping for breath, frequently pulling off their masks as the winds blew the gas away.

One survivor later told a reporter, "I thought I was safe and took off my mask to drink some water. In seconds my throat, eyes, and skin were burning."

"Mommy, am I going to die?" That heartbreaking question from a little girl may have broken the tense silence inside the second-story family room, where adults told the children, "Play with your toys."

During lulls in the tear-gas attacks, cult members attempted to carry on their daily routines. Because the FBI had shut off the water and electricity some days before, cult members bathed in collected rainwater, then saved that same water to wash their clothes later in the day.

Outside, the tear-gas attacks resumed. As if anticipating some action, an ambulance, with lights flashing, rushed toward the compound. But once again no one emerged from the building. Authorities had already notified Hillcrest Baptist Medical Center in Waco to be on the alert.

By then it was 9:00 a.m. Tank drivers continued pumping tear gas, while adrenalin pumped through their own veins. This time the large battering arm ripped into the second floor of the compound. Minutes later another tank punched a hole into the back wall of the building, sprayed an infusion of tear gas, then immediately withdrew.

◆◆◆

The physical pain and emotional trauma that the Davidians must have experienced seemed only to strengthen their resolve. They believed that they were involved in something much larger than a showdown in Waco, Texas. To them it was Armageddon—the catastrophic end of the world. And to their minds, to retreat would mean forfeiting their eternal salvation.

Having obeyed David Koresh thus far, they determined to stick by him until the end. He had been their conscience and their guide. They firmly believed that he would lead them to victory, and so they let his agenda control their thinking. However, David Koresh, who quoted voluminously from the writings of Ellen White to his flock of mostly former Seventh-day Adventists, had conveniently omitted one of her often-repeated counsels: "It is not God's design for any human being to yield his mind to another human being" *(Mind, Character, and Personality,* vol. 2, p. 706).

Koresh had demanded the money, wives, time, and minds of his followers, and they had willingly given their all. Through mind-control techniques common in prison camps, he had accomplished a level of "thought reform" that might better have been called brainwashing.

◆◆◆

Whether at the instigation of Koresh or some of his beleaguered followers, observers noticed some indication of a desire for peace on that fateful morning.

At one point a cult member appeared at the front door of the ranch, waved his arms, and retrieved the telephone. Ten minutes later a white sheet hung out of a second-floor window. "We want our phones fixed," the scrawled message read.

The FBI tried frantically to reconnect the special phone, but their attempts to reestablish communications proved unsuccessful. And without agreement on a temporary cease-fire, no one dared cross the line to talk.

The FBI continued blasting the compound with tear gas from the tanks. By this time they had knocked the front door out. Cult members responded to each battering attack with rounds of gunfire.

Inside the compound emotions continued to run high. At 10:00 a.m. a cult member once again stood in the doorway, this time waving a white flag.

"Is this a surrender signal?" the FBI boomed over the loudspeaker. But to that fateful question came no reply.

◆◆◆

Survivors have since spoken of those last hours. David Koresh took charge, leaving his third-floor bedroom to check on the women and children. He walked the debris-filled halls one last time as he checked gas masks and exercised his familiar control. Those who knew him well spoke of his ability to submerge the will of his followers into his own irrepressible convictions.

What turned out to be the final assault began around noon. Once more a tank lumbered toward the building and rumbled right through the front door. The clapboard walls rocked on their foundations as kerosene lamps crashed to the floor. The huge propane tank situated near the front door dislodged and blocked several exits.

Once again cult members responded with gunfire. Confused and probably scared, many Davidians sought shelter in the interior of the cavernous complex. Fleeing the gas, women and children clustered in the center of a second-floor room, from which there was no exit.

The old wooden building trembled and shook with each blow of the tanks. Bales of hay hauled into the rooms to provide a buffer from the bullets also provided some protection from the chilly Texas spring.

Koresh, having made what turned out to be his final rounds, gathered his inner circle once more in a room of cinder-block construction. However, one of the M728 tanks pierced that room also and began pumping in tear gas.

"They gathered in a central area where the gas was minimal," said FBI official Jeffrey Jamar, on-scene operations commander. "The people who were inside were in such absolute control very few resisted any instruction until the very end."

Exactly what happened next we may never fully know. According to the FBI, Koresh, cornered and desperate, gave his last order as the Branch Davidian "messiah." Obedient as always, the Mighty Men moved quickly to carry it out.

At 12:17 p.m. FBI snipers claim to have seen a grim-faced man in a second-floor window make a throwing motion. A fireball followed.

Surviving cult members say the group had no mass suicide plan and that tanks knocking over the lanterns started the inferno.

Regardless of what or who actually started the fire, ominous black smoke rolled out. Simultaneously, puffs of smoke and flames curled upward from perhaps two other areas of the compound.

Some survivors reported that cult leaders raced through the compound, shouting, "The fire's been lit! The fire's been lit!"

Outside, horror-stricken FBI agents shouted over the loudspeaker, "Don't do this to these people. This is not the way to end it!"

But within a matter of minutes, wind-whipped flames

engulfed the building and with it more than 80 men, women, and children.

Nearby witnesses reported blood-curdling screams, and some thought they heard shots. Overcome by smoke inhalation, cult members crouched on the floor of the building and gasped for air. Ammunition began to explode. High winds continued to fan the flames. Huge billows of smoke rose from the complex of interlocking buildings.

"They're killing themselves," one onlooker cried, echoing the shock felt across the nation.

The FBI made sporadic rescue attempts, but hampered by smoke and massive explosions rocking the compound and the unbearable heat, they were largely unsuccessful. However, a few cult members did jump from windows or dash through other openings to safety.

One man, spotted on the roof, signaled that he did not want to be rescued. Finally, his clothing in flames, he fell from the roof. One woman emerged from the holocaust with her clothes on fire, only to try to walk back into the flames. An agent rushed in and grabbed her.

But most of those who died were never seen again after the flames began to lick out of a tower window just after noon. As the fire spread, explosions continued to rock the compound as ammunition stores blew up. It took less than 30 minutes for the fire to completely level the compound. By 12:21 the wooden four-story watchtower, lookout for the last shift of black-clothed sentries, collapsed.

◆◆◆

The FBI did a quick body count of persons escaping from the compound. Nine.

Traffic screeched to a halt on Interstate 35 as passengers poured from their cars to watch the inferno. The flames and thick black smoke were visible five miles away from Ranch Apocalypse.

Back in Michigan the distraught parents of Jeff Little, like other parents and family members of cult victims, sought comfort and prayers from their local church pastor and compassionate friends.

The death of Pat and Lonnie Little's son, and of so many others, captured on camera for the world to see, brought with it a black cloud of depression and despair more choking than the smoke that had floated up from the debris.

In Anaheim, California, Ruth Mosher spoke of an earlier premonition. Somehow she had known she would never see her daughter, Sherri Jewell, alive again.

Sandy Hayden, a close friend of Sherri's, shared the same feeling based on a recent phone conversation with Sherri. "She said everything was going to be OK," Sandy confided to a reporter. "I kept asking if she was going to kill herself, and she'd say, 'It's only flesh,' and I knew."

The devastating fire may have come as no surprise to cult family members, but it totally surprised the FBI.

"The setting of fires in the compound brought about a tragedy that none of us expected," said an official FBI spokesperson. "None of us expected them to commit suicide."

The FBI had based their projections on a professional psychiatric analysis of Koresh's past behavior. The FBI believed Koresh to be personally vain and fearful of bodily injury. This picture of Koresh, drawn from an incident during the siege, turned out to be tragically false. At one point Koresh reportedly had armed himself with grenades and signaled his intention to have a final shootout with the FBI, commit suicide, and go out in a blaze of glory before the eyes of the world. But after a tearful goodbye to his children and followers on the inside of the compound, Koresh changed his plans. In the eyes of the FBI and the psychiatrists upon whom they relied, the incident outweighed other evidence, such as Koresh's repeated references to a fiery end and the misplaced but ardent religious zeal with which he and his followers held to their mission.

A statement made by Karen Doyle, one of the Branch Davidians outside the compound, served as an example of just how strong that commitment was. "I wish I could have been there," she lamented. "That's where the truth was." But the federal agents just couldn't comprehend that kind of dedication.

◆◆◆

Now only ashes remain of Ranch Apocalypse. Fire trucks began dousing the smoldering rubble with water while ammunition still continued to explode. As the last embers of the fire simmered and sizzled, many people now wondered how such a tragedy could have happened.

First and foremost in their minds were the questions: Why did innocent children have to die? How many people had been in the compound? And might David Koresh have possibly escaped?

For Seventh-day Adventists other questions came to the fore, including why so many former Adventists had perished in the compound. Perhaps something important could be learned from this experience. Once the fire cooled, many of these questions would be resolved as grim-faced investigators sifted through the ashes of this painful experience.

Chapter Three

Sifting Through the Ashes

By dawn Tuesday all that remained of what once had been known as Mount Carmel were smoldering heaps of ruin and a ghostly, scorched water tank. A small concrete bunker still stood, surrounded by the charred and twisted rubble of what was once a 50-room complex.

Carefully a few dozen workers picked through a maze of twisted wiring and stacks of canned goods. Small orange flags, marking the location of bodies, fluttered around the site.

◆◆◆

It seemed that everyone was trying to make some sense of the tragedy. The gruesome search for victims drew comments from nearby neighbors, far-off relatives, and people around the world. "I cried today for those poor little darlings who didn't even have a chance," said Vernice Baker, a great-grandmother from the Waco area. "When you think of those children, you think of your own."

◆◆◆

Harold Wiley looked up as two Chinook helicopters roared overhead. Then he stared off into the fields surrounding his small home. "It was time for it to be over," he said quietly. Then he hesitated. "Someday," he began again slowly, "it will all be back to normal around here—just a nice, boring, quiet place."

◆◆◆

Some onlookers, such as the FBI and most of the nation, reacted with shock and horror. For others, the inferno only confirmed what they always believed would happen.

Sherri Jewell's daughter, Kiri, shed no tears as flames razed the Texas compound where she had left her mother behind.

"This is what [cult members] told her was going to happen," Kiri's aunt explained.

"She is probably more matter-of-fact about this than any of us," said Kiri's father, David Jewell. "She has said from the very beginning that there was no possibility that this was going to be ended peacefully."

◆◆◆

Down under, in Melbourne, Australia, the fretful sleep of Bruce and Lisa Gent, former cult members, ended abruptly the Tuesday morning after the Ranch Apocalypse fire. When the phone rang in their home, the long-awaited news from the Texas compound couldn't have been worse.

"I just lost my whole family. Two kids and two grandkids," Bruce said. "This is just unreal."

The Gents' 24-year-old daughter Nicole and her two young children, fathered by David Koresh, had perished in the flames. Nicole's twin brother, Peter, had died earlier in the February 28 shoot-out.

"They were all prepared to die for Koresh," Lisa Gent said of her children.

◆◆◆

Other family members of persons inside the compound had long ago resigned themselves to the idea of a violent outcome. They had seen the stranglehold that David Koresh had on the minds of his followers and knew firsthand the frustration of attempting to change the mind-sets of those who'd surrendered their wills to him.

Lonnie Little remembered his visit to the compound several years earlier, when he had wanted to free his son Jeff.

"Don't cast your pearls before swine," Koresh had told Jeff in the presence of his father when both sensed that Lonnie wouldn't join the cult. But after the daylong visit, the father had felt that he must leave immediately or risk recruitment himself.

Lonnie had climbed into his car and sat for a long time looking at the light shining from Jeff's bedroom, the back end of a broken-down school bus.

"I didn't think I'd ever see him again," he said later.

For Jeff and Sherri, long indoctrinated by Koresh, the answer was simple. Whatever David Koresh said, they did. The strategy employed by Koresh, of a surrendered conscience, flew right in the face of the "little red books" from which he so often loved to quote.

◆◆◆

"I have spoken distinctly regarding the dangerous science which says that one person shall give up his mind to the control of another. This science is the devil's own" (*Mind, Character, and Personality,* vol. 2, p. 704).

In addition to its use in prisoner-of-war camps, fanaticism often employs mind control. A fanatic, according to *Webster's Ninth New Collegiate Dictionary,* is a person "marked by excessive enthusiasm and often intense uncritical devotion."

In the eyes of most Americans, David Koresh, along with many of his followers, fit the description to a tee. After all, promiscuity, child abuse, mind control, and stockpiling weapons aren't exactly normal characteristics of mainstream American life!

◆◆◆

Long before the standoff in Texas, Koresh's idiosyncrasies had caused a permanent parting between himself and the Seventh-day Adventist Church. Once a baptized member, Vernon Howell (later David Koresh) claimed to have new light regarding the seven seals. Unfortunately, his new light contradicted the Seventh-day Adventist traditional interpretation of Revelation, and when church officials pointed that out, thus rejecting Howell's prophetic views, he became angry. Eventually the local congregation had to disfellowship him.

The former ties of both Koresh and his followers already posed a difficult public-relations problem for the denomination. If David Koresh had had his name on the Seventh-day Adventist Church books at the time of the standoff, the unflattering headlines about the denomination would have been even more severe.

Family members of people who died in the Davidian complex, for the most part, reacted negatively to the teachings and lifestyle of David Koresh.

"David Koresh wasn't a normal man. I never trusted him," said Oliver Gyarfas, whose granddaughter Aisha Gyarfas died in the fire. Then he added the shared opinion of many familiar with the situation: "The people inside were brainwashed."

As relatives, friends, the news media, and the nation contemplated the grisly tragedy, commentaries and opinions popped up everywhere. Some church groups defended the cults, saying that they deserved tolerance. In fact, a broad cross-section of religious organizations issued a joint statement cautioning the government against clamping down on religious cults such as the Branch Davidians.

The joint statement, spurred by the planned government investigation into the violence at the compound, stated that "although investigation is appropriate, we oppose the attempt to define what is a valid religion or set the parameters of a proper church."

However, Bible-believing Christians would probably agree that religious freedom, as important and necessary as it is, is never an excuse for violent or criminal conduct that harms others or threatens public safety.

The Seventh-day Adventist Church issued its own statement in response to the fire at Ranch Apocalypse: "Although the Seventh-day Adventist Church has no affiliation with the Branch Davidians or any other cult, our hearts go out to those who have lost loved ones in the Waco, Texas, tragedy. As compassionate, peace-loving people, our prayers are with these families.

"The Adventist Church provides an array of services and programs which focus on Christ's caring model of meeting the needs of those around Him. These services and programs include: a worldwide network of hospitals, clinics, and mobile health-screening vans; an international disaster relief agency to help victims of hurricanes, floods, tornadoes, and other disasters; and the world's largest Protestant school system."

In Dallas a religious researcher named Frank Leahy brought forward a document that he had written previously after an exhaustive review of Koresh's teachings. After reviewing hundreds of passages of Scripture cited by Koresh, Leahy concluded that Koresh actually believed that he was a divinely appointed prophet. According to Leahy, Koresh had totally convinced his followers that his way was the only way to salvation. That his answer was the only truth that mattered in their lives.

The final, terrible proof was the fact that Koresh had overwhelmed even a mother's inbred instinct to protect her children. It had not been strong enough to dissuade her from the cult's chosen path. And so the babies—the innocents—died also.

The violent ending had no possibility of a peaceful resolution, according to Leahy's analysis. Koresh taught that a set number of martyrs must die for Christ from the beginning of time until the apocalypse. When that specific number of martyrs is complete, the end would come. (Some reports say that Koresh set the magical martyr number at 20 million, then later changed it to 10 million.)

Since in their eyes the Davidians were the only true believers, they were also the only eligible martyrs. When the Davidians died for Koresh, they would fill up the sum, Koresh would be resurrected, and his followers would slaughter the unbelievers.

Based on these beliefs, it is reasonable to believe that if the FBI didn't kill Koresh and his followers, he was determined to make martyrs of himself and his followers as a self-fulfilling prophecy.

According to another singular prophetic interpretation, the Branch Davidians believed that during the last apocalypse final events would divide into segments of certain lengths of time. Since the bloody shoot-out took place on February 28, Leahy calculated that Koresh believed an end to the world would occur on or about April 18.

Survivors of the inferno later reported that Koresh was under pressure to prove that what he had taught was right, through the fulfillment of his prophecy. By forcing the final showdown on or around April 18, the government certainly played into his hands and probably strengthened the resolve of his devotees to follow him to the bitter end.

As we mentioned earlier, the psychological profile of Koresh developed by FBI behavioral specialists appeared to preclude the possibility of suicide. The FBI based it on Koresh's apparent fear of being hurt—reflected in his backing out of the plan to blow himself up with grenades—and all his talk about the future. His call to 911 when the shoot-out first began also might indicate that he had no thought of suicide—at least not at that time.

Some experts aren't sure Koresh really intended to commit suicide, whereas others contend it was definitely in the plan.

"Suicide is against my religion," Koresh had stated at one point in the negotiations. He also showed an unflagging interest in what would happen to him if he should emerge from the compound. "I'm too young to die in here," he told FBI negotiators in another conversation. And Koresh and Steve Schneider reportedly had their lawyers auctioning rights to their story for figures as high as $2.5 million.

One key obstacle to Koresh's surrender was his fear of being raped in prison, his lawyer commented. "Wouldn't you be concerned if somebody said you're going to be identified and publicized as a child molester?" attorney Dick DeGuirin asked.

As for Waco cult members holed up within the compound, they reasoned that if they left the compound, they were, in fact, giving up their beliefs and would be damned forever.

"They believe they're part of a matter that's much greater than just simple life and death," one Waco resident observed. "To them their decisions will affect their souls."

Judy Schneider, one of the cult members, received a serious injury to a finger during the initial shoot-out. Over the telephone doctors advised her that she should come out and receive immediate medical attention at the hospital, or else gangrene might set in.

Instead Judy suggested to the horrified doctors that perhaps she should just cut off her finger.

The FBI, whether it realized it or not, was dealing with very committed people—people who really believed in what they were doing, even though their lives were in jeopardy.

The Christian world considers a high level of commitment desirable for any believer. The Bible says: "Be thou faithful unto death, and I will give thee a crown of life" (Rev. 2:10). Koresh undoubtedly quoted the passage to his followers.

Unfortunately, his followers made the ultimate sacrifice for an unworthy man and an unworthy cause—largely due to the mind control prowess of David Koresh. Mind control for the Branch Davidians seemed to reduce or eliminate the fear of death, and even give them license to kill.

One Los Angeles man told reporters, "The night I met Koresh

. . . he asked me, would I die for Christ? I said, 'I guess so.' He said, 'Would you kill for Him?' I said No. He turned to my friend and said, 'Hey, you just brought me another weak Christian.'"

Koresh knew his hypnotizing effect on his followers and used it to his best advantage, teaching that he was the lamb of Revelation—the only one who could open the seven seals, thus setting loose catastrophic events that would end the world and propel the group to heaven. He set himself up as "God." A "divine" Koresh had the right to control his followers and exact obedience from them.

As their leader he believed that he was fathering the children who would later rule the world. He also promised his male followers perfect spouses in heaven—taken from the rib of each man—and that each man and his wife would have their own planet to populate.

According to the research done by Frank Leahy, Koresh and his followers took as absolute truth the following:

• Koresh was the reincarnation of Jesus, whom they believed was the reincarnation of David, king of Israel. His followers were the "chosen people" to which the Bible refers.

• They were exempt from civil laws because they followed God's higher law. The strict discipline of children, Koresh's multiple sex partners, and the cult's armament all had biblical precedents.

• The Bible foretold everything that had happened to them, including the investigation by the Bureau of Alcohol, Tobacco, and Firearms, the February 28 attempt to serve a search warrant, Koresh's wounds, the FBI's decision to bombard the compound with sounds, and what Koresh viewed as the authorities' slanders against him.

• The siege was one of the tribulations described in the Old Testament apocryphal book of Baruch, from which Koresh sometimes cited. Each tribulation lasted seven weeks, meaning theirs would end on or about April 18.

• Anyone who worshiped on Sunday was of Satan rather than of God.

• The Bible not only allowed but demanded that the Branch Davidians be deceitful with such outsiders, including their attorneys and federal negotiators.

• God wished Koresh to be sinful according to the world's standards so that humankind would find him more approachable than Jesus, who was perfect.

• By revealing the meaning of the seven seals of the book of Revelation, Koresh would destroy the followers of Satan, including the government and organized religion. Koresh believed that he had opened five of the seven seals, and to open the sixth seal he and his followers must die.

• Their deaths would involve a great fire, which would consume the forces of Satan arrayed against them.

These points, which the Davidians took as absolute doctrine, seem totally absurd to the rest of the world, even to other Christians. And even the Davidians had moments of doubt.

According to Paul C. Looney, an attorney for Louis Alaniz, the Houston man who sneaked into the cult compound in Waco on March 26 and emerged weeks later, a number of Koresh's followers appeared dubious of their leader's claims. They expressed their reservations during free-flowing discussions that were a regular feature of life inside the surrounded compound.

"They told Koresh they needed to see some kind of sign so that they could verify that he was a prophet before they could endorse him as a prophet, and he prophesied there would be an earthquake and a breaking of the dam," Looney said. "Time passed, and it didn't happen, and more and more people were beginning to say, 'David, this has not happened.'"

Looney explained that some of Koresh's followers decided that if Koresh's prophesies didn't come true by May 14, which marked the group's second Passover observance, they would leave.

While Louis Alaniz never believed that Koresh would surrender, he was convinced that the bulk of his followers would, Looney said.

After he left the Branch Davidian fortress on Saturday, Alaniz told the FBI about the growing rift between Koresh and some of his followers.

◆◆◆

Investigators picked their way through the rubble and charred remains scattered over the city-block-sized compound. The majority of bodies were found facedown, indicating a probability of death by smoke inhalation. But then as time wore on, the startling discovery of bodies with bullet wounds deepened the already dark mystery of what had really happened inside the compound during those final hours.

To even begin to understand what happened, or why it happened, one must first look at the childhood of David Koresh.

Chapter Four

Always Looking for Something

Little Vernon Howell clung to the handlebars of his two-wheeler, pedaling with all his might. Tears streamed down his dusty cheeks as he pursued the speeding car ahead of him. When the car disappeared in a cloud of dust, so did Vernon's dream of living with his grandmother, Erline Clark.

That vanishing car represented just one link in a chain of disappointments in the youngster's life, each centering around a continued absence of or rejection by any potential male role models.

◆◆◆

David Koresh was born Vernon Wayne Howell to an unwed teenager on August 17, 1959. "I was born because my momma and daddy had a feeling between them," Vernon later told a friend. "There was never any love there."

Both the emotional stress that his mother, Bonnie, must have experienced during pregnancy and the prenatal foundation of an empty family situation presented just the first of many setbacks for the little boy.

Vernon's father, Bobby Wayne Howell, and Bonnie lived together for two years, but never married. During that time, family members reported, both Vernon and his mother suffered physical abuse. Then Bobby Wayne Howell fell in love with another woman and left home for good. That was Vernon's first rejection.

The second rejection came because of the intense shame and condemnation Bonnie suffered because of the birth of her illegitimate son. Affected deeply and emotionally by the terrible stigma, and not much more than a child herself, she found herself ill-equipped to cope with the responsibilities of parenthood. Bonnie loved little Vernon and wondered how best to ensure a happy life for him. So she did what she thought was best—she gave him up. The girl placed Vernon in the care of her mother, Erline Clark. Erline took in her grandson and then quickly added to the family two children of her own—Sharon and Kenneth Clark. They grew up with Vernon, more as siblings than aunt and uncle.

"Vernon was bright and precocious," Erline told a friend. But Vernon's grandfather was never affectionate with his stepgrandson, nor was he expected to be, because he was a hard-drinking macho man, country-type Texan.

The apparent lack of interest shown by his grandfather (except when it came to discipline) marked a third painful rejection for the young Vernon, who was not yet 5 years old.

During the three years that Vernon remained in the care of his grandmother, Bonnie Clark visited periodically, masquerading as his aunt. But in 1964 she fell in love with and married Roy Haldeman, and reappeared into Vernon's life to introduce herself as his mother. She took Vernon away from the woman who had met his needs and whom he had called "Momma" for more than half his young life.

"I was shocked and confused," he later told his followers. "Here I was just 5 years old, and my whole world was turning upside down."

This fourth major upset in his life must have made a significant contribution to the insecurity that Vernon manifested in later years. But now back with his real mother, he at least hoped to enjoy his new "dad." However, the new stepfather soon had his own son to worry about, Roger.

"Roger was always the favorite," Vernon said. "I was always getting whopped by Roy for everything, while Roger got away with murder. When I acted up, when I had a bad report card, I got my tail whomped."

Vernon's low grades were partly the result of a learning disability that he later claimed was dyslexia. Because he was always behind in his schoolwork, his school put him into a special class reserved for slower students.

"I got teased every day. They called me 'retard, retard' and '4-eyes' because I have glasses," Vernon later told a friend.

Although being teased must have been terribly hard on him, even worse was the rejection he seemed to face at every turn of his young life.

Although Vernon's mother sent him back to live at his grandmother's when he was 14, the youngster failed once again to win the affection of his grandfather.

"Vernon seemed always to be wanting acceptance and love by the men in his life, and it never seemed like he got what he was looking for," a relative observed later.

The boy seemed to be looking for love everywhere, especially from a father figure, but the love he craved eluded him. The young man's natural need for a consistent male role model went unfulfilled, and most would agree that its lack may have deeply affected his later life.

"What the child sees and hears is drawing deep lines upon the tender mind, which no after circumstances in life can entirely efface" *(Mind, Character, and Personality,* vol. 1, pp. 150, 151).

The physical abuse Vernon suffered as an infant preceded his later sexual trauma. On several occasions he told his followers that when he was 6 an older girl molested him, and that also when he was a teenager a group of boys sexually attacked him in a barn. It seems likely that the unfortunate experiences of his childhood contributed to his later obsessions with sex and violence, as well as an obsessive-compulsive habit of masturbation, which was common knowledge in the Davidian compound.

Although no one would attempt to justify what Vernon Howell became in his more mature years, when one considers the tangled chain of rejections, the early childhood physical abuse, and later incidences of sexual abuse, his obsessions with control over others and his environment do seem a little more understandable.

◆◆◆

In addition to the alleged physical abuse as a young child, Vernon received what many would consider today as harsh physical punishment from his stepfather.

The practice of physical punishment was not, of course, limited to the Haldemans' home. It was very much part of Protestant America, and rural Texas was no exception. For centuries Protestants have been among the most ardent advocates of physical punishment.

Larry Christenson, whose book *The Christian Family* sold more than 1 million copies in 1970, wrote: "The scriptural method of discipline is simple and unequivocal: the rod."

Dr. James Dobson, a modern-day advocate of physical punishment, once spoke of pain as "a marvelous purifier." Dr. Dobson, whose child-rearing ideas Seventh-day Adventists widely respect, used the imagery of battles in his book *Dare to Discipline* in advising parents to "outlast" their children in order to gain obedience.

Author Roy Lessin went even further in his book *Spanking: Why, When, How?* "Spanking is God's idea," Lessin wrote. "He is the one who has commanded parents to spank their children as an expression of love. Spanking is not optional. It is an issue love cannot compromise."

Protestants cite a number of Old Testament texts in support of this view. One of the strongest is Proverbs 23:13, 14: "Withhold not correction from the child: for if thou beatest him with the rod, he shall not die. Thou shalt beat him with the rod, and shalt deliver his soul from hell."

However, punishment without love often accumulates a host of pent-up emotions within the child. According to child psychiatrists, such emotions often emerge in later life—in the form of anger, obsessiveness, rigidity, anxiety, apathy, depression, paranoia, sadomasochism, aggression, and domestic violence—wreaking a vengeance on anyone close to the former victim.

It was evident throughout the bloody ordeal at Waco that both the grandmother and mother of David Koresh cared for him a great deal. However, it seems that the abuse he suffered from his father during the first two years of his life, the two incidents of sexual abuse that he personally related, and the repeated incidents of rejection and stern physical punishment by his stepfather and grandfather without accompanying communication of any love or encouragement, may very well have contributed to later evidence in his personality of nearly all the psychological symptoms listed above.

Punishment without love is ineffective. And physical discipline as a normal result of everyday infractions, although perhaps accepted by the mainline Protestant world, goes against the counsel given to Seventh-day Adventists: "If milder measures prove insufficient, punishment that will bring the child to its senses should in love be administered. Frequently one such correction will be enough for a lifetime" *(Child Guidance,* p. 250).

Seventh-day Adventists stand in danger of being influenced by the rest of the Protestant world, which places too much emphasis on the Old Testament texts admonishing physical correction and not enough on the tenderness of Jesus toward children, shown in the New Testament.

Another hallmark of Protestant discipline throughout the past several centuries has been the desire to break the will of a child.

"From the seventeenth century to the present, evangelical and fundamentalist Protestants have persistently advocated the crushing of the will even before a child can remember the painful encounters with punishment that are always necessary to accomplish such goals" *(Spare the Child,* p. 65).

John Robinson, a minister in the 1600s, reflected the general belief of the day when he wrote: "Children should not know, if it could be kept from them, that they have a will of their own" *(Spare the Child,* p. 66).

Jack Hyles, a popular Christian author in the 1970s, wrote that "spanking should be administered firmly. It should be painful, and it should last until the child's will is broken" *(ibid.).*

Later Christian authors have tried to differentiate between breaking the will and breaking the spirit of the child, saying that punishment must continue until the parent has broken the will but not the spirit.

Yet Ellen G. White spoke of guiding the child to obedience, not breaking the will. "The will is the governing power in the nature of man, bringing all other faculties under its sway. . . . Every child should understand the true force of the will. He should be led to see how great is the responsibility involved in this gift. The will is . . . the power of decision, or choice" *(Child Guidance,* p. 209).

The experience of Adolf Hitler offers an infamous example of what happens when a father attempts to break the will of his child. Hitler, who suffered numerous severe beatings nearly every day of his childhood, treasured up a storehouse of hate that he later, when given the opportunity, unleashed on the world.

Evidently the same harsh discipline that affected Hitler so deeply and contributed to the later tyrant he became was practiced commonly throughout Germany at the time. It has been suggested that this unloving discipline not only prepared Hitler for his grisly career, but also set up the German people to follow him. They had been trained to give unthinking, submissive obedience from their youth up. Most did not think for themselves, and quite possibly did not know how. Having been raised in such authoritarian homes, they perhaps craved an authoritarian leader who would tell them every move to make.

Although many factors could have influenced Koresh's followers to choose his rigid, demanding rule, an authoritarian background could have been one of them that prepared them to want someone to dictate to them in every factor of their lives.

If there is one lesson to be learned from this situation—and there are many—it is that we must teach our children to think for themselves.

And perhaps if Vernon Howell had received a little more guidance and a little less discipline, he would not have developed the headstrong, rebellious attitude that became his trademark.

◆◆◆

As he grew to his teen years, Vernon became bored with school. He attended Dallas SDA Junior Academy for a while, but dropped out for good in the tenth grade after feuding with a teacher.

"He was having a lot of trouble at home with Bonnie and Roy," his aunt recalled.

After years of disappointment in school and with personal family relationships, Vernon struck out on his own. During those years, friends say, he was often overwhelmed by a massive sense of guilt that manifested itself in wide mood swings.

"One minute he believed he enjoyed a special and unique relationship with God. The next minute he considered himself to be worthless," reports Marc Breault, a former cult member.

Those strong feelings of guilt were evident even in his childhood. It's quite likely that he felt to blame not only for the rejection by his father, stepfather, and grandfather, but also for being shuttled from home to home.

Bonnie Haldeman, Vernon's biological mother, remembered that "he would often pray for hours, kneeling by his bed crying and praying."

Vernon's grandmother backed up the story that he frequently knelt for hours and prayed to God in a way that few adults could understand. Vernon's family took such behavior, which to a trained counselor might have evidenced the extreme guilt he felt, as a manifestation of his devout nature.

Despite his learning disability, Vernon was blessed with a photographic memory. One of his proud early accomplishments was his memorization of the entire New Testament by the age of 12.

Vernon's life did have some bright spots. His aunt, Sharon Clark, with whom he grew up, remembered many happy times when her family and the Haldemans visited back and forth. However, each visit invariably ended with a crying, heartbroken Vernon, who begged to return and live with "Momma," his grandmother.

Back and forth, back and forth, Vernon's life was never under his own control. From birth to age 2 he lived with his biological mother. Years 2 to 5 he spent with his grandmother. Then age 5 to 14 he once again lived with his biological mother and stepfather, Roy Haldeman. During those nine years, he always longed to return to his grandparents. Finally he got his wish at age 14, only to be kicked out by his grandfather two years later.

I'm always the extra wheel, he must have thought.

This troublesome child seemed destined to live with rejection by the men in his young life. "There was never a really good male role model for him—someone who really took an interest in him and genuinely wanted to spend time with him and teach him something," his aunt Sharon said.

The many rejections that Vernon experienced seemed to fuel his drive in later life to continually fill that void with religion, beer, women, guns, and one of the loves of his life—hard rock music.

CHAPTER FIVE

MOTOR CITY MADMAN

You're hot. You're sweaty. Pulse racing. Mouth dry from exertion. Eyes darting side to side.

"Your thumb strokes the flint in your right while your left practices making a power-thrust fist.

"The house goes dark!

"The pulse comes from all sides. FORWARD FISTS and LIGHTERS UP!!!—READY—TWO—THREE—I-G-N-I-T-E!!!

"It's bone-crunching loud, and you feel one with the Motor City Madman, and that is the way it should be, 'cause tonight you are going to ROCK!"

So goes a Detroit *Free Press* article describing the music of rock star Ted Nugent.

Vernon Howell idolized Nugent, the Detroit-based star known also as the "Motor City Madman." The fascination began at a young age. Vernon's typical teen-decorated room, a remodeled shed in the backyard of his grandparents' home, included black lights and walls plastered with Ted Nugent posters.

"There never was a good male role model for Vernon," his aunt, Sharon Clark, has observed.

But Vernon found himself a role model, and he found it in Ted Nugent, although he also listened to the music of other rock artists as well.

Nugent, a frequent host at Detroit's Cobo Hall New Year's Eve "Whiplash Bash" extravaganza, earned his reputation for heavy metal combined with violent hunting videos.

For Nugent, who described himself to the *Free Press* as a "responsible predator," relaxation at home meant lounging with friends in camouflage shorts and with a pistol in his pocket. "Even in the midst of all this," he told a reporter as he pointed to his numerous hunting trophies, "me and my dead friends have learned to relax."

If you have never heard Nugent's music, you can get a fairly good sense of it through his own less-than-humble description: "You will not experience anything in your lifetime, outside of sex and the birth of a child, that compares to what these rock-'n'-rollers feel when I do my hunting songs."

Rock music and guns were two of the twin fascinations that captivated Vernon in later life, and it is possible that the music of Ted Nugent introduced him to the combination.

◆◆◆

By 1978 Vernon was 18 years old and facing an uncertain future. He used his handyman skills and worked in construction, finally scraping together enough money to afford the down payment on a new Silverado pickup truck.

The black vehicle with red velour interior became Howell's pride and joy, and he kept it full of rock tapes featuring Eddie Van Halen, Aerosmith, Eric Clapton, and Ted Nugent.

"He was a typical teenager," said Debbie Owens, who counted herself lucky to be dating Vernon.

A conventional rocker, Vernon taught himself to play the guitar, and he carried it everywhere he went. He often set up his amplifier in an open-air pavilion next to a swimming pool and played his music until he would "zone out," Debbie said.

"It was like nothing else existed when he played, unless he messed up," she went on. "Then Vernon was supercritical of himself. A real perfectionist about chord changes.

"That was his main thing in the world. I was second—music came first," Debbie told a reporter.

He formed a rock band during his teenage years, but no one can remember a single paying gig.

Vernon also mixed rock and religion. Sometimes he practiced his electric guitar, with the volume turned up full blast, late into the night. Finally he would stop playing and reach for his Bible.

◆◆◆

When Vernon was 17 years old he attended the Adventist church in Tyler, Texas, for a time. During his association with the church he confided in one of the elders, Harvey Bockman, his intense feelings of guilt over his lifelong devotion to rock music.

"He wouldn't even touch a guitar," Bockman said. "They [the rock songs] implied very strongly to him that he was under a satanic influence, so he had washed all that away."

During that time Tyler members say that Vernon became very strict, often condemning in others what he'd formerly done himself. The Holy Spirit must have been working with him, but he seemed trapped on a roller coaster between extremes.

Vernon picked out faults and sins in others and often confronted fellow church members about their "sins."

Ginger Fry, whose husband, Ed, was a classmate of Vernon, vividly remembered one incident. Vernon confronted her during an intermission at a church social after she'd performed in a bluegrass band. "Vernon practically called me a whore because I was wearing blue jeans," Ginger told *USA Today.* He also accused her and her husband of playing the devil's music.

This habit of judging others, unfortunately, had little lasting impact other than alienating Vernon from his fellow church members.

Perhaps he was only trying to learn a lesson that has always been difficult for many conservative Christians, including

Seventh-day Adventists: "We must learn to place the best possible construction upon doubtful conduct of others" *(Mind, Character, and Personality,* vol. 2, p. 789).

◆◆◆

Despite Vernon's efforts to give up his music and have a new experience in Christ, the burdens of guilt carried from childhood, and the lure of the world around him continued to attract him. He left the Tyler SDA Church, grew his hair long again, and with his guitar at his side, headed for greener pastures. Seeking fame and fortune as a rock guitarist, he tried to make it professionally both in Texas and California.

The exact role rock music played in the shaping of Vernon Howell into David Koresh may never be known. However, for the rest of his life heavy metal continued to form a major part both in his lifestyle and in his recruitment and later mind control of followers.

One thing is for certain: The type of music a person listens to does affect that person, and the music of choice tells something about both the person listening to it and society.

"To hear music is to respond to it . . ." wrote Paul Hamel in his book, *The Christian and His Music.* "When we are within hearing distance of music we are powerless to keep it from registering in our bodies" (pp. 25, 26).

Rocker Bob Dylan agreed. "A song is an experience," he wrote. "The guy who writes the song and the guy who sings it each feel something; the idea is to get you to feel the same thing or something like it. And you can feel it without knowing what it is."

According to Dr. Hamel, music can affect respiration, circulation, blood distribution, blood-sugar ratio, pupillary reflexes, metabolism, and brain-wave patterns.

"Martial music played by marching bands serves a larger purpose than simply adding glitter and lively music to parades," he wrote. "The martial music imparts to the marchers the emotional strength to walk farther and faster than they would normally be able to. Since martial music appeals to the strong emergency emotions, it is as effective as the injection of a stimulating drug."

Sherri Jewell and Jaydeen Wendell, two of Koresh's ardent later followers, must have sensed this when they composed marine-style cadences for the cult women to exercise by:

"We're with Cyrus;
He's our man,
Gonna kill his enemies
Where they stand.

If you have
The world's desire,
Gonna throw you
In God's holy fire."

Many see nothing detrimental in the beat of modern music, but they do recognize much harm in the lyrics of secular rock. The lyrics of heavy metal bands, of which Vernon was so fond, deal with such topics as the death of God, sitting at Satan's left hand, human sacrifices, and sex with corpses.

Lonnie Little, "treated" to a mini-concert during his brief visit to Ranch Apocalypse, had two things to say about the music of David Koresh.

First, if you weren't strapped into your seat when he started, he would blast you right out of your chair!

Second, the lyrics were definitely vulgar.

It's unclear how many rock stars and performers actually practice satanism, but according to some Christian sources, satanists own as many as 85 percent of today's heavy metal bands.

Because the average teenager listens to 10,500 hours of some form of rock music between grades 7 and 12, one can understand James Dobson's comment: "It is difficult to underestimate the negative impact music is having. Rock stars are the heroes, the idols that young people want to emulate" (Neil Anderson, *The Seduction of Our Children,* p. 90).

"Music influences kids," wrote Dr. Paul King, a child psychiatrist in Memphis, Tennessee. "The kids I've seen who are violent and into drugs by and large are into heavy metal. . . . The lyrics become their philosophy" *(ibid.).*

At the present, probably no rock star wields as much influence as Madonna. Madonna has been banned from MTV (not exactly a bastion of morality), blasted by the Vatican, and almost arrested for simulating masturbation onstage. Recently she released a provocative film detailing her controversial behavior during her "Blonde Ambition" tour. In the film, she alluded to the connection between her music and satanism. "I have a lot of demons inside me," she lamented. "My pain is as big as my joy."

Vernon Howell developed an obsession with Madonna in addition to his fixation on Ted Nugent. At one point, he even claimed to have heard a voice from heaven, which said clearly, "I will give thee Madonna."

At one point Vernon took a trip to Hollywood along with Marc Breault and Steve Schneider, two of his top lieutenants. With the help of millionaire Paul Fatta, Koresh purchased huge amounts of musical equipment—and he bought only the best. He had a collection of about 15 guitars, both acoustic and electric. Two of his favorites he nicknamed "Adam" and "Eve."

Koresh wanted Steve Schneider to contact Madonna's music managers and convince them that Koresh was the best thing to happen since the Rolling Stones. Steve was to pose as a big-time manager who'd handled lots of big stars. According to Marc Breault, the assignment daunted even the irrepressible Steve Schneider, although he did manage to speak with someone high up in Madonna's organization.

The resounding no from Madonna's managers did nothing to faze Koresh's ambitions. One of his prophecies was that Madonna would eventually come into his arms and take her rightful place in his assortment of "wives" known as the "House of David."

Koresh's unique mix of religion and rock showed up via heavy gold-colored business cards, featuring the word "Messiah" on the front in thick, black, one-inch type. The *i* in Messiah was dotted with the Star of David, and a highly symbolic sword made a dramatic slash through the name. In addition to the word "Messiah," the cards said "David Koresh, guitar, vocals, and Steve Schneider, Music Manager." The card listed no addresses or phone numbers, but Koresh got his money's worth by listing nine Bible verses on the back.

He was always on the alert in Hollywood, trying to lure musicians to "return with me to Texas and play for the Lord." Once he treated singer Sheridan Stewart to one of his seductive recruiting sales jobs in a Los Angeles rock music club. Telling Stewart that he believed in giving women a more active role in religious life, he sprinkled his sales spiel with numerous biblical references. Stewart later commented that Koresh was impressive, but she wasn't buying. She didn't want to sing in a band with a man who thought he was Jesus!

But Koresh had occasional successes in luring musicians like David Thibodeaux and Jaime Castillo, young drummers tired of life in the Los Angeles fast lane, who wanted a more spiritual existence while pursuing their music.

"He was impressed," Thibideaux's mother later told a reporter. "There was a charismatic, electrifying personality."

Koresh wooed Marc Breault (who later escaped the cult and wrote an insider's view of life among the Davidians) with the promise of mixing music and ministry. Breault played keyboard in Koresh's rock band, even though their big plans to win converts with music eventually fizzled.

Although he never made it to Hollywood or even Texas stardom, Koresh was a star at Ranch Apocalypse. When playing his rollicking riffs of heavy metal for cult members, he usually stood at the center of a stage in an auditoriumlike building that his followers had constructed. He often wrote and played his own compositions.

In a sense, rock music must have been the language of

Koresh's own rebellion. Perhaps he was reacting against the lack of control he must have felt in his childhood, against the rejection he so often experienced, or against society in general. Whatever he was trying to say, he found perfect expression in his music.

"In a sense, all rock is revolutionary," *Time* magazine once observed. "By its very beat and sound it has always implicitly rejected restraints and celebrated freedom and sexuality. The music of rock is vulgar, rude, and deliberately offensive. It is the ideal vehicle for protest" (Jan. 3, 1969, p. 49).

During the 51-day standoff at Ranch Apocalypse, Koresh often responded to the raucous noises blared over FBI loudspeakers by staging mini-rock concerts at a moment's notice.

"They would play their terrible sounds, and David would just go in and crank up the generator and would play the guitar," said one of the men who sneaked into the compound during the standoff and was later released. "The other brothers would be playing the drums, and David would be singing to the stars." The performances strained the electric generators that the cult was forced to rely on after authorities cut the power to the compound on March 12.

With regard to being captivated by rock music, the words Koresh penned to the FBI might better have been applied to himself and his followers: "Fear me, for I have you in my snare."

◆◆◆

In the painful aftermath of Waco, the Seventh-day Adventist Church and we as individuals might do well to reconsider our attitudes toward soft rock and religious "vege-rock" music. It seems entirely possible that our acceptance of certain forms of music opens the door for more advanced expressions of the same form.

"There is evidence that the more a person listens to music, the more strongly it affects him," Paul Hamel wrote. "This is especially true with the extremes in music. It can become like a drug, with the addict needing larger and larger quantities. Just as the drug abusers crave more and more potent drugs, so do the devotees of jazz and rock seek an increasingly intemperate kind of music as time goes on. . . . Each succeeding generation of popular music fans needs something stronger for the creation of the desired kick or wallop."

"I call it narcotic music, the hard-rock stuff," commented one of the Branch Davidian's California neighbors about what he heard from the nearby cult premises.

Our bodies have a built-in rhythm, according to Lloyd Nedley, a former pop music artist and GM engineer who spends much of his spare time warning people about the dangers of the music he used to play. The overpowering beat of rock and some other forms of popular music go against the rhythm of our bodies, and that is what makes them sensual. The beat bypasses the frontal lobe of the brain, where we make judgments, going directly to the emotional part of the brain.

The purpose of this book is not to judge music, but in the case of rock music to trigger thought and further study. When we started to write this book, one of the pastors we spoke to advised that we might run into some hard questions when studying the events at Waco but that we should not be afraid to tackle them.

We can have no doubt about the type of influence that rock music had on David Koresh or the role it played in his life. But did Adventist indifference to softer forms of rock open the door to heavy metal? If the beat of the music actually does have a sensual effect, as research suggests and even verifies it does, should we not reconsider the use of soft rock even with religious lyrics?

And would Koresh's Adventist recruits, many of whom were attracted to him by a shared love of rock music, have been more protected from his mind control if they had not listened to his music?

"It [rock] was nothing but beat, smashed and crunched and hammered home like some amazing stampede," wrote one rock enthusiast. "You were only left with chaos, beautiful anarchy. . . .

The sound destroyed you, raped you regardless, and you had no defenses left."

If you didn't know that this quote was talking about rock music, you might think it was describing the mind-control tactics used by David Koresh.

Chapter Six

Six-shooter Junction

Waco doesn't like being called Six-shooter Junction, although the nickname still might fit. After all, it's part of the legendary land of the Texas Rangers, where the hard-riding, hard-shooting lawmakers tamed their portion of the Wild West.

During the 1800s brash young cowpokes often adopted Waco as their own nickname. Shoot-outs became so common in the rowdy town that it later served as the setting for dozens of Hollywood horse operas.

Today Waco residents would prefer that others recognize their city of 104,000 for its 14 museums, fine zoo, excellent educational facilities, and mainstream Protestant ethic. But one of those museums is the Texas Ranger Hall of Fame, and Waco continues its dubious reputation, which it shares with the entire state of Texas. You are more likely to be killed by a gun in the Lone Star State than you are to die in a traffic accident.

Most of Texas evidently has a totally different attitude toward guns. Many Texans viewed the Ranch Apocalypse raid as an invasion of Koresh's home, and Texas residents have long defended their right to use force, if necessary, to ward off any unwanted intrusions into their homes. Although what Koresh and the Davidians did was certainly not legal, it sparked more sympathy in

Texas than it probably would in any other state. A parade supporting Koresh even marched through Dallas!

More than 16,500 Texans, including some police officers, own machine guns. And according to Texas law enforcement agencies, the 17 million Texas residents own a grand total of approximately 60 million firearms—an average of about three guns per person.

One staunch Texan summed up the attitude of some of his comrades when he declared, "If someone had come climbing in my window, I would have blowed them away too."

Not all Texans feel this way, however. Seventh-day Adventists in particular have long been known for their noncombatant role both at home and abroad. Branch Davidians were also known as a peace-loving, nonviolent people—until the unfortunate takeover of their leadership by Vernon Howell.

Under Vernon's leadership the Branch Davidians amassed a disproportionate number of weapons. The Ranch Apocalypse arms arsenal was believed to include Ruger mini-14 rifles, capable of firing as many as 750 rounds per minute if automatic; AK-47 assault rifles, capable of firing 600 rounds per minute; Israeli submachine guns; .223-caliber semiautomatic rifles; Beretta semiautomatic pistols with 15-shot magazines; 9 mm Glock handguns; a .50-caliber machine gun; and hand grenades.

In the words of one journalist, "It was an astonishing array of firepower."

Why would David Koresh need all those weapons? Two possible scenarios come to mind. One would be for the "divine slaughter" of Seventh-day Adventists, first envisioned by the Houteffs, early leaders of the group that evolved into the Branch Davidians. The Davidians felt that God would call upon them to purge the Seventh-day Adventist Church in a violent way. Although no evidence has surfaced that the Davidians actually intended to initiate violence, some have speculated that such a plan might have been in place and could even have been one of the sparks that encouraged the failed ATF initiative.

The second might be that the Branch Davidians may simply

have felt that they were preparing to defend themselves against any potential aggressors.

Whatever the case, the massive arms buildup on Ranch Apocalypse became the object of a federal investigation, thanks to concerned family members around the world.

◆◆◆

Vernon was not violent as a child, according to his aunt. "The worst thing Vernon ever did as a child was blow up a frog with firecrackers," she said.

Although we couldn't use the frog as evidence that Vernon had a violent nature early in childhood, some research suggests that cruelty to animals can be the first step toward later acts of abuse toward humans.

As a child Vernon did, like many Protestant Americans, receive physical punishment. He in turn used the same methods of discipline on those later under his control, according to countless reports from former cult members. Vernon often administered verbal spankings and other reprimands when followers either made a mistake or displeased him in some way.

Lonnie Little remembers one such instance that happened during his brief visit to Ranch Apocalypse. During the Sabbath morning service cult members took turns reading the Bible. Vernon listened intently to each of his followers. With his photographic memory, he could quickly detect when one of the readers misread or stumbled over a word.

"I'd like you to start that over," he'd say in a quiet authoritative voice, and the unfortunate individual would have to start all over again, as well as endure the sighs of fellow listeners, who might have been growing impatient with repeated restarts.

Whatever level of verbal violence Vernon may have subjected his followers to, it was only a replay of the death-and-life being continually emphasized in our violent society.

Vernon's early obsession with Ted Nugent's "hunting music"

no doubt influenced the cult leader in a desire to collect all types of guns. He was also a video fan and insisted that his followers watch certain hand-picked films for their own trips into vicarious violence.

Former cult member Robyn Bunds told FBI agents that Koresh had members watch "extremely violent" Vietnam war movies, telling them they were training films. Koresh, she said, always slept near a weapon.

Also it was reported that Koresh had a desire to equip remote-controlled model airplanes with explosives—turning them into flying bombs.

◆◆◆

In looking for roots to his violent behavior, we must also consider that television shows and cartoons may have influenced Koresh as a youngster.

The increasingly hot issue of children and violence on television is being looked at even by secular experts. Many are concerned that instead of treating our children as our most precious national resource, we have allowed them to be regarded as a commercial market via TV programming and commercials.

Certainly many children have played with guns as youngsters as well as watched hundreds of hours of cartoons and haven't grown up to be violent. Genetic makeup, personality type, and environmental factors all play a part in the reaction of children to what they see and hear. But more than 200 studies about TV and film violence confirm the evidence that viewing violence encourages violent behavior.

"The character of Napoleon Bonaparte," Ellen White wrote, "was greatly influenced by his training in childhood. Unwise instructors inspired him with a love for conquest, forming mimic armies and placing him at their head as commander. Here was laid the foundation for his career of strife and bloodshed. Had the same care and effort been directed to making him a good man, imbuing his young heart with the spirit of the Gospel, how widely different might have been his history" *(Child Guidance,* p. 196).

When children of today view violent television programs and play with weaponlike toys, they are learning a habit-forming behavior structure that encourages fighting to win and the spirit of domination.

According to *Boys Will Be Boys,* a thought-provoking book that discusses the role of toys in shaping our children, today's toys encourage assault, murder, racial violence, and rape as well as militaristic attitudes. Some of these toys are teaching such values to children as young as 18 months old!

Many teachers also now express concern that more and more children are obsessed with war play, which evidently erodes the teachers' control in the classroom.

Because of the captivating nature of TV cartoons, many parents see little danger in letting their children watch them. But more and more young people, like David Koresh one day did, are acting out their violent fantasies in real life.

◆◆◆

After the Waco fire, a leading clergyman stated that the downfall of the Branch Davidians was David Koresh's obsession with women, rock music, and guns.

Authorities estimated that Branch Davidians spent nearly $200,000 accumulating their high-powered arsenal in just 16 months and were preparing for a "military-style operation" in Waco in which "all nonbelievers would have to suffer."

But how could a group of devout people who lived quietly and peacefully outside Waco for 40 years turn so potentially violent?

According to Derek Davis, a professor of religion at Baylor University: "The Waco Davidians' apparent misfortune was to become dominated by Mr. Koresh and his messiah fantasies. He turned them around: a rigidly pacifist sect, under Koresh's control they began to stockpile weapons. They also condoned behavior they once considered immoral."

Changes in leadership "do not usually rise until the prevailing order has been discredited," wrote Eric Hoffer. "The discrediting is not an automatic result of the blunders and abuses of those in power, but the deliberate work of men of words with a grievance" *(The True Believer,* p. 119).

In other words, if Vernon Howell had not arrived on the scene, George Roden might have ascended to leadership despite his frequent blunders.

"Where the articulate are absent or without a grievance," wrote Hoffer, "the prevailing dispensation, though incompetent and corrupt, may continue in power until it falls and crumbles of itself" *(ibid.).*

The prevailing power of the Rodens did crumble. The Branch Davidians put their faith and trust in David Koresh and also chose to listen to his music. The music of David Koresh—heavy metal—has long been associated with violence. Disturbances at rock concerts have been common and sometimes deadly throughout the years, as participants drummed themselves into nearly uncontrollable frenzies. In comparison, one could hardly imagine such a disturbance at a "Back to Bach" concert!

◆◆◆

When Koresh made violence an element of his prophecy, the Branch Davidians went along. After all, they had been predicting for years that the world would end with a divine slaughter of Seventh-day Adventists. Koresh rationalized that he was preparing his followers for an end-of-the-world showdown with law enforcement, thus justifying his hellfire philosophy.

During the year before the siege the self-described lamb of God oversaw the buildup and storage of weapons and ammunition that filled an entire room—stacked to the ceiling. For some time he also had insisted on having an armed guard patrol the compound 24 hours a day.

In the compound high-powered rifles lay near children, who saw growing up in terms of the weapons they would one day carry. When a state welfare worker went to the compound to investigate allegations of child abuse in February 1993, a boy of about 7 told her that he wanted to grow up because then he would be issued a "long gun" like all the adult men.

When the worker went back to the compound later, Koresh told her that he was a messenger from God, that when he revealed himself, last year's Los Angeles riots would pale by comparison and that there would be a "military-type operation."

One of the unifying agents leaders use to solidify their movements is hatred. "Mass movements can rise and spread without belief in a God, but never without belief in a devil," wrote Hoffer (*ibid.,* p. 86).

Adolph Hitler understood the importance of an adversary in solidifying power and motivating his cause. At one point Hitler was asked whether the Jew must be destroyed. "No," he replied, "we should have then to invent him. It is essential to have a tangible enemy, not merely an abstract one" *(ibid.).*

Some sort of common hatred evidently evokes a feeling of kinship. Communist Russia saw its "devil" in the United States. Earlier revolutions regarded their enemy as the current ruling class. David Koresh and the Branch Davidians visualized their enemy in the ATF. In addition to the ATF, Davidians saw another adversary in the Seventh-day Adventist Church, for whom they predicted a "divine slaughter."

Some in Adventist circles have speculated that the Davidians intended to instigate and carry out this "divine slaughter" themselves, since they felt that was their scriptural role. Koresh's statements about future military-type operations and eclipsing the violence of the Los Angeles riots certainly added fuel to such surmisings, although we may never know the full story.

Historically, the "unifying enemy" for Christians has been the devil. Yet the creation of a devil for Christians to hate was certainly not part of God's overall plan, no more than sin was. As a matter of fact, Christians are encouraged to concentrate on the good and pure in the Bible, not on the devil.

When Christians make an enemy out of another church, the government, or some individual who happens to disagree with their doctrine, it seems likely that they are expending their energies in the wrong direction. Perhaps leaders of such groups are really using these tactics more as a unifying or fund-raising method, since the real enemy of God's church is none other than Satan himself.

"For we wrestle not against flesh and blood, but against principalities, against powers, against the rulers of the darkness of this world, against spiritual wickedness in high places" (Eph. 6:12).

But why does hatred serve as a unifying factor? Perhaps it expresses a desperate effort to suppress feelings of inadequacy, worthlessness, guilt, and other shortcomings. Self-contempt becomes contempt of others, and individuals suffering from it make persistent attempts to justify the hatred. One effective way of doing so is to find others who hate as we do (see *The True Believer,* p. 88).

"Often, when we are wronged by one person, we turn our hatred on a wholly unrelated person or group," Hoffer observed *(ibid.)*. Hitler, abused in his childhood, unleashed his revenge on the Jews. Russians, bullied by Stalin's secret police, found it easy to detest capitalist America. David Koresh, who suffered rejection in his childhood, avenged himself in numerous ways in his adulthood.

"True hatred springs more from self-contempt than from a legitimate grievance," Hoffer wrote *(ibid.,* p. 89). Perhaps, in the case of David Koresh, his inability to accept himself, coupled with inordinate guilt, fueled the self-contempt that led him to lash out at those around him and at the world.

Although hatred is a convenient instrument for mobilizing a movement, it does not come cheap. Those who harbor hatred lose "all or many of the values" they originally "set out to defend" (see *ibid.*, p. 91). For the Davidians, one of those values was the sanctity of life itself.

And the FBI, which had dealt with killers, terrorists, assassins, and thousands of other violent criminals in the past, found it incredibly difficult to deal with the weapons and apparent hatred of the holed-up Branch Davidians.

Chapter Seven

❖

Roller-coaster Religion

It was Sabbath in Richardson, Texas, and Pastor Phil Payne was about to address his congregation for the last time. Having accepted a call to another church, he felt some apprehension as he glanced up and out over the congregation.

His eyes blinked in surprise as a well-dressed and extremely attractive elderly lady, followed by nine other people, entered. Pastor Payne immediately recognized the woman dressed in a striking blue dress and bonnet as none other than Lois Roden, leader of the Branch Davidians.

"Why today?" he murmured to himself. Lois Roden had never popped in to hear his sermons before, but the Branch Davidians and their leader did have a well-earned reputation for disrupting church services.

With a great deal of apprehension, Pastor Payne proceeded with his sermon. Much to his relief, the expected disruption never came.

After the service ended, Pastor Payne noticed young Vernon Howell talking with Lois Roden in the parking lot. It was really no surprise, for even at that young age Vernon had a reputation for talking religion for hours to anyone who would listen.

An extremely intelligent young man, Vernon knew his Bible better than most and carried it with him virtually everywhere he went. Pastor Payne remembers Vernon as a mild-mannered, kind young man, who showed tremendous care for others ostracized by the church.

Perhaps that was because of the distance he had sometimes felt between himself and the other more well-to-do members of the Richardson congregation. Vernon Howell didn't fit in that well to the social order of things, although he got along as best he could.

Even at his young age Vernon felt a certain affinity for Christ. Maybe this was why he adopted his religion in such a zealous manner. For Christ, not unlike Vernon, had been born to an unwed mother. Christ encountered comments about illegitimacy, such as the ridicule by some Pharisees who told Him that they knew who their father was.

Sometimes unkempt, sometimes dressed quite attractively, Vernon had a certain charisma that intrigued others. Pastor Payne remembers Vernon from camp meetings. In between meetings, Vernon would sit and strum his guitar, playing songs for the young people who gathered around him.

But on this Sabbath in Richardson Vernon was interested in something other than music. He was talking to Lois Roden.

Pastor Payne doesn't know the exact turns Vernon Howell's relationship with the Branch Davidians took from then on, but he did know that Vernon began spending some time with the Davidians at what at the time they called Mount Carmel.

From then on, Pastor Payne usually saw Vernon at camp meeting. Sometimes the young man showed up alone, sometimes with the Davidians.

As for Vernon's religious experience, it seemed to fluctuate back and forth between extreme, Bible-carrying religiosity and lapses into the love of his life, hard rock. At camp meeting Vernon was usually in a more religious frame of mind.

"The songs I heard Vernon play at camp meeting would not come near rock," Pastor Payne recalls. "Vernon would play songs that would be accepted in most churches."

◆◆◆

When he was about 17, Vernon began attending the Seventh-day Adventist church in Tyler, Texas. Although the Branch Davidians had influenced his thinking he still seemed open to the Adventist message and was experiencing a renewed fervor in his religious life.

Just months before, his Dallas girlfriend had become pregnant. Vernon evidently loved the young woman and wanted to marry her, but the girl's father would have none of it. After this heartbreaking rejection, Vernon began attending an evangelistic series at the Tyler Seventh-day Adventist Church.

"He was going through a chastising," his aunt Sharon said, seeking atonement for the guilt he felt over his sexual appetite.

"I'm having a hard time keeping these thoughts out of my head," Vernon told her.

"He prayed a lot, and he lost a lot of weight," was the way she remembers it.

From the first day that Vernon walked into a midweek prayer meeting, reported Bob Bockmann, now an elder in the Tyler church, Vernon commanded attention. Although his discussions of Scripture were sometimes obscure, it was still nice to have a young man who was serious about the Bible.

The Tyler congregation was delighted to see a young, apparently fallen-away member return to the faith. When members learned that Howell was out of work, Harriet Phelps, an elderly woman whose sons were grown, offered him a room in exchange for work around her farm.

Bockmann and his wife, Maggie, befriended Howell, and Bockmann said that the young man seemed to be burning with guilt over his past sex life and with resentment that he had not been permitted to marry his ex-girlfriend.

"The girl he was with in the Dallas area was about to have his baby," Bockmann said. "It was just killing him, because her parents didn't want him around anymore. He really missed the girl and felt terribly rejected that he wasn't able to be with her."

He said that Howell also professed to have intense feelings of guilt over his lifelong devotion to playing rock music. "He would not even touch a guitar," Bockmann reported. "They [the rock songs] implied very strongly to him that he was under a satanic influence, so he had washed all that away."

At first, Bockmann said, Howell seemed receptive to the church's teachings. "He said, 'I'm just a newborn baby.' Here was a point where he was asking to be led, asking to be counseled. Sad to say, it was very short-lived."

Vernon, excited about his reconversion, let his newfound fervor get the better of him. The Seventh-day Adventist Church was already known for its strict moral values. Yet the reformed Vernon suddenly became everyone's judge, especially when it came to the conduct of women, telling at least one father that his daughter was "wearing what he thought was immodest dress." Bockmann says that "he became very straitlaced."

Apparently anything Vernon did, he did with great vigor. Dan Buckingham, head elder of the church at the time of Howell's reconversion, told how the young man reacquainted himself with the five-book Conflict of the Ages series.

"I know this for a fact," Buckingham said, "that Vernon shut himself up in a room in the home where he was staying and read those books night and day until he had completed the entire set, only coming out for his immediate physical needs."

But Tyler members became concerned when Vernon seemed able to command such rapt attention from younger church members. He would stand in a corner and "all-encompass them," said deacon Hardy Tapp's wife, Annette, "and just totally take over the conversation."

And although struggling with his feelings of sexual guilt, Vernon used the church to develop both platonic and sexual relationships with women. "He alluded that he was attracted to me," recalled one church member, who was much older than Vernon.

She said that he would speak to her for hours about his childhood, often tearfully recounting physical abuse. Once, she said, he showed her a pattern of burn scars on one leg that he said had resulted when someone had forced him to kneel on a heat register.

His younger aunt, Sharon, said she believes that this period was the last best chance for anyone to have interrupted Vernon Howell's transformation into David Koresh. However, at this point, Vernon had already deepened his involvement with the Branch Davidians, joining them as they attended Texas camp meetings and aggressively distributing their pamphlets.

"I saw him there passing out literature with the Davidians while he was still in his teens," remarked Dan Buckingham.

The Davidians had a unique interpretation of the book of Revelation, believing that a special prophet would come to them, and that prophet alone would be able to open the seven seals of Revelation.

◆◆◆

In the meantime Vernon became captivated by a Revelation Seminar series sponsored by the Seventh-day Adventist Church. The seminars, conducted by Jim Gilley, featured dramatic images in a multimedia portrayal of Armageddon.

Gilley is a rousing speaker, and his video representation of the Apocalypse—featuring earthquakes, pestilence, and religious persecutions—combined with video material of current events that pointed toward the imminent millennium.

"We went every night of the week," Sharon said.

Vernon couldn't stop talking about the details, which seemed to bring all his years of Bible study into focus.

"Vernon said that even Mr. Gilley had a piece of the puzzle missing," Sharon Clark said of the discussions about the book of Revelation. The missing piece, Vernon told her in earnest, was the seventh seal, something that only a new prophet could open. (The seven seals, as described in the book of Revelation, bind a scroll held in God's right hand that is supposed to prophesy the calamities preceding the end of the world.)

Because Davidian theology could be built only on Adventist theology, you had to have an Adventist understanding of the Bible even to understand what the Davidians were talking about. Taking advantage of this, they portrayed themselves as teaching a deeper understanding of the Bible than currently available through the Adventist Church. Caught up in his overwhelming zeal and yearning for a more meaty knowledge of the Bible, Vernon had come to agree with and publicly defend Davidian doctrine.

Sharon said that Vernon was convinced that it was time "to have a new prophet and a new light" in the Seventh-day Adventist Church, and that he was quite possibly that person.

"Vernon was claiming prophetic status even as a teenager," said Dan Buckingham, head elder of the congregation at that time.

"There is a moment in the career of almost every faultfinding man," wrote Eric Hoffer, ". . . when a deferential or conciliatory gesture from those in power may win him over to their side. At a certain stage, most men of words are ready to become timeservers and couriers" *(The True Believer,* pp. 121, 122).

Could Vernon's time with the Tyler church have been the last best chance to reach him? According to Dan Buckingham, he and others spent many hours with Vernon in an effort to work things out.

Jim Gilley said in an interview that Howell approached him one night and offered to help expand the video effects of his evangelistic series. Gilley rejected the offer because of the expense involved.

Vernon tried hard to bring his message to the Tyler congregation, interrupting sermons on a number of occasions to share his views in an often lengthy way.

"If you make a disturbance like this again," Dan Buckingham remembers telling Vernon as he and two deacons escorted the young man out after one particularly loud incident, "I will personally call the police."

By this time the Tyler church members had all they could take. In 1981 the Tyler Seventh-day Adventist Church formally disfellowshipped Howell. Although doctrinal differences were the primary reason, Vernon's continued advances toward married young women or underage girls had also contributed to the action. Following his formal rejection by the church, Vernon gave his full allegiance to the Branch Davidians.

"That's when it took off," Sharon commented. "That's when he really became serious."

◆◆◆

"He was always looking for something," said Kenneth Clark of Vernon's earlier life. "He had his rock; he had his women. But it was never enough."

"He wanted to be loved," Vernon's grandmother later said. "Maybe it's something he's always needed—to have a group of people he could care for."

Looking back on it now, Pastor Payne wonders, like many others, what he might have done differently. Now a hospital chaplain with training in psychiatry, Pastor Payne says he wishes that he had known the meaning of some of the warning signs in Vernon's behavior back then.

The Richardson and Tyler churches had tried to reach him, but somehow Vernon found in the Branch Davidians a sense of family, a feeling of acceptance, and a place where he could excel.

And against the Seventh-day Adventist Church he nursed a personal grudge, which no doubt fueled his wholehearted support of the complaints harbored against it by the Branch Davidians.

"However much the protesting man . . . sees himself as the champion of the downtrodden and injured," wrote Eric Hoffer, "the grievance which animates him is, with very few exceptions, private and personal. His pity is usually hatched out of his hatred for the powers that be" *(ibid.,* p. 122).

Unfortunately for Vernon Howell and the Branch Davidians, their joint mission and the union that resulted was to become a fatal attraction.

CHAPTER EIGHT

PREPARATION OF A PEOPLE

Vernon Howell crouched behind a broken-down car and trained his assault rifle at arch-rival George Roden. After years of searching, he had found a home, a family, and a religion that he was willing to fight and die for. He had found the Branch Davidians, and only George Roden stood in his way.

Long before Vernon arrived on the scene, the Branch Davidians had broken off from the Seventh-day Adventist Church and formed their own religion. Their original leader, Victor Houteff, joined an Illinois congregation in 1918, and later served in a lay leadership role in the Los Angeles area.

Houteff remained in the church for 16 years but, following a doctrinal dispute, formed a separate religion, which he named the Shepherd's Rod. He asserted that God had appointed him to "cleanse" the denomination of false believers. Also he informed his followers that God would soon set up His true church in Palestine. There Houteff would serve as Christ's lieutenant.

Through much of their troubled history, the Davidian group has clung to a peculiar interpretation of the book of Ezekiel. In one particular passage God sends an angel to place a mark in the foreheads of the righteous inhabitants of Jerusalem. This mark would spare them from invaders that would destroy the city.

The Shepherd's Rod interpreted Jerusalem to be the Seventh-day Adventist Church, the few righteous were the Shepherd's Rod, and the destroying angel would enter the ranks of the church. As a result, the Shepherd's Rod felt that they had a special message for Seventh-day Adventists. Operating with evangelical zeal, they took their beliefs directly to Adventist congregations.

Common tactics included distributing pamphlets in parking lots, buttonholing the faithful after services, and warning that denominational leadership was corrupt.

"They prey in a very parasitic form on Adventist churches and Adventist members. . . . They feel that the modern Adventist Church is an apostate," said Bill Shea, a Seventh-day Adventist researcher. "So the relationship has been one of ongoing antagonism."

Shepherd's Rod followers also invested their leader with great authority. Leaders held prophetic status, with the unique ability to open the seven seals referred to in the book of Revelation and to interpret the contents of the seals correctly.

In 1935 Houteff moved to Waco, Texas, and built the original Mount Carmel center on 189 acres of rolling hills. By 1940 the center stretched across 377 acres and housed 64 believers.

Houteff believed that the restoration of David's kingdom in Palestine was imminent, and he changed the name of his organization to Davidian Seventh-day Adventists to reflect that belief. But his death marked the beginning of a period of turmoil for the Branch Davidians. His wife, Florence, succeeded him as the cult's prophet. She predicted that a "divine slaughter" of Seventh-day Adventists, complete with the resurrection of Victor Houteff, would occur on April 22, 1959. At that time the Davidian kingdom would supposedly be reestablished.

At the news of this prediction, hundreds of followers joined the group, disposing of their property and businesses. Membership swelled to nearly 1,400.

About that time the Davidians sold their property to the city of Waco, Texas, and moved to the present property about 10 miles east of Waco.

The year 1959 came and went, and the divine slaughter never occurred. All but 450 loyal members left the compound, and those 450 split again, with the largest group following rival leader Ben Roden. Roden took control of the compound and dropped the words "Seventh-day Adventist" from the Branch Davidians' name.

Ben Roden, who taught that he was the antitypical David, king of Israel, died in 1978, and his eloquent, matronly wife, Lois, succeeded him. Lois claimed to have a vision from God in which she saw that the Holy Spirit is the feminine aspect of the Trinity. To proclaim this message, Lois started a magazine named *SHEkinah,* which developed a substantial circulation worldwide.

The Christian world recognized the intelligent and popular 70-year-old as a globe-trotting ambassador for her church. She traveled extensively and mixed freely with the rich and famous.

According to Martin King, a reporter who confronted David Koresh inside the Waco fortress, "Lois Roden was on first-name terms with many famous American preachers and Christian entertainers, including Pat Robertson, Jim Bakker, Jimmy Swaggart, Jerry Falwell, Sandi Patti, and Keith Green. It wasn't just the rich and famous either. There were the infamous, too, such as the then president of the Philippines, Ferdinand Marcos."

It was soon after Lois Roden became the Branch Davidian leader that Vernon Howell, searching for deeper meaning to the Scriptures, found the group. Attracted to Lois, Vernon was amazed at the people she knew within the Christian world. As the editor and publisher of *SHEkinah,* Lois had widened her circle of influence as well as the magazine's circulation.

Vernon, with his polite manner and immense knowledge of the Bible (particularly of the book of Revelation), made an immediate impact on the Davidians—and on Lois!

Although he knew Scripture and could convincingly quote text after text, he wasn't at first as readily accepted as he might have liked to be. Some cult members felt that he was not only opinionated but arrogant. But Vernon, being the incredible survivor that he was, managed to worm his way into the hearts and minds of the Branch Davidians, and Lois.

One day, according to reports from former cult members, Vernon approached the elderly woman and claimed to have had a vision. "'And I went unto the prophetess; and she conceived, and bare a son,'" Vernon quoted from Isaiah 8:3.

The two, although sort of an "odd couple," became lovers, and Vernon used the relationship as a stepping-stone toward leadership in the cult.

George Roden, until this time the heir apparent to the leadership, came across as being eccentric. He just didn't have the popular appeal Vernon did, and Vernon saw his opportunity. In addition to Lois's friendship, Vernon also befriended Perry Jones, a high-ranking Davidian official whose daughter he later married.

Vernon's direct maneuvering toward Davidian leadership did not escape notice. A brawling bear of a man with a thick beard, George Roden hated Vernon. George knew of the intimate relationship between Vernon and his mother, and claimed that Vernon had raped her. He determined that Vernon's ambition would not interfere with his own plans to take over the cult.

As George, a huge hulk of a man with a 10-gallon hat and a .38 revolver on his hip, hated Vernon, Howell returned the favor. In a less-than-affectionate manner, they nicknamed each other "Tub of Lard" and "Mosquito," respectively.

However desperately George wanted the job, Lois remained adamant that her eldest son was not fit to take over leadership at Mount Carmel. And Vernon was often privy to their heated arguments.

Soon Vernon made his move, letting his desire for control be known openly. According to reporter Martin King, "Both men realized that what they were fighting for was absolute control of the hearts and minds of hundreds of people. Not only that, but they were also vying for control over millions of dollars in cash, property, and assets held by the Branch Davidians throughout the world. As leader, they would not only have direct control of the assets all around them, but they would also have the power to demand contributions from loyal followers wherever they might live."

Thanks to Vernon's growing influence, the Davidians found themselves torn between his leadership and that of George Roden.

In 1984 Roden forced Vernon from the compound at gunpoint. At that time most of the cult members followed Vernon to Palestine, a town in east Texas. There they built and lived in 8' by 12' wooden boxes and plotted their return to Mount Carmel.

Lois Roden finally died in 1986, leaving her son in full control of the compound. In his quest for undisputed leadership, Roden challenged Vernon to a sort of messianic duel—a test of divine powers. He proposed that the man who could bring back to life the dead body of Anna Hughes, an elderly woman who had been buried on the compound for more than two decades, would be the undisputed leader of the Branch Davidians.

Roden dug up the remains, and Howell promptly asked the sheriff to arrest Roden for corpse abuse. When the sheriff demanded proof, Howell and seven men staged a commando-type, predawn raid to steal the body.

Hearing a commotion, Roden appeared with his Uzi and engaged Vernon Howell and his seven, later known as the "Rodenville Eight," in a shoot-out. No one was injured, although the tree behind which big George took cover was filled with bullet holes. After the two-hour gunfight, it was Howell and his comrades, not Roden, who were arrested. Taken to jail, they were charged with attempted murder by the authorities.

During the subsequent trial Howell's followers shouldered the casket containing the remains of the former Branch Davidian into the McLennan County courtroom.

"The judge disallowed it as evidence," said Waco attorney Gary Coker, who represented Vernon Howell, "but all the jurors saw it."

Vernon Howell and his seven were never convicted, in large part because George Roden was then serving six months for harassing the courts. He had filed legal motions asking God to give AIDS and herpes to the Texas Supreme Court judges!

During Roden's leadership the Davidians had gone to the

state's highest court to challenge a Waco court's ruling about the tax-exempt status of some of their acreage. In addition to asking God to wreak vengeance on the Texas Supreme Court, Roden also spewed hatred toward the people of Waco throughout the document.

"The religious prejudice is so thick here in Waco that you can cut it with a knife, so to speak," Roden wrote. "The hatred against me and my organization is so explosive here that it is at the exploding point as a pressure cooker about to blow.

"I guess when you have a big religious town there is bound to be religious intolerance of other unpopular religions just as it has been down through the ages," Roden continued, ending with "Every religious entity has been in its beginning a cult."

Possibly disgusted because of the inflammatory language of Roden, Waco lawyer Lyndon Olson, Sr., who had handled the case, withdrew from the engagement. Olson later declined to specify his exact reasons for withdrawal, although they seem fairly obvious.

In other court motions the Davidians seemed a little more gracious. They claimed to be "in the benevolent work of restoring people and families to viable citizenship and taxpaying citizens and taking them off the welfare rolls. . . . This not only reduces the government welfare programs and burdens," they went on, "but lessens the crime rate."

But the cult's tone changed again dramatically in a later filing, just weeks before the shoot-out between Roden and Koresh. "What does the Texas Supreme Court think they are, God? . . . Maybe God will make it up to you in the end and send you herpes and AIDS, the seven last plagues, and shove them up your . . . Then maybe you will, and the rich . . . as well in the world, get your just deserts you have been itching to get for so many years during the oppression of the blessed poor," the motion said.

The motion, routinely denied by the Supreme Court of Texas, ended by saying: "Thank God we still remain by His grace.

Rehearing requested . . . by you . . ."

Although Vernon's maneuvering, relationship with Lois Roden, subsequent marriage to Rachel Jones, and personal charisma helped win him the undisputed leadership of the Davidians, the bizarre behavior of George Roden had also most certainly helped his case.

In 1987 Vernon wrote a rock song about Roden, which eerily enough sounded like a prophecy of his own future:

> "There's a madman living in Waco.
> Please, please, please won't you listen?
> It's not what it appears to be.
> We didn't want to hurt anybody,
> Just set our people free.
>
> In the night of the darkness
> We're risking our lives for the Lord.
> We're helping our women and children
> Into their houses restore.
>
> There's a madman in Waco
> Bowing his knees to Baal.
> Won't you help, Mr. Sheriff,
> So we won't fail?
>
> This is for the little children,
> God knows how it should be.
> Stars and stripes are flying.
> Give us justice and liberty.
>
> There's a madman living in Waco
> Praying to the prince of hell.
> Won't You help us, Lord, now,
> To pay our bail?"

After the mistrial regarding the gunfight between Howell and Roden, a jubilant Vernon and his followers invited all the jurors to a party. The jurors accepted the invitation, and seemed charmed by the friendly defendant. He served them nonalcoholic beer and vegetarian pizza.

Later the authorities charged Roden with the murder of a 56-year-old man. Roden admitted killing the man, whom he believed had been sent by Vernon Howell. "I shot Wayman Dale Adair in self-defense, since he told me he was sent by Vernon Howell to Odessa. I believed that he was sent there to kill me," Roden testified.

Found not guilty by reason of insanity, Roden was locked in a state mental hospital. With his challenger under lock and key, Vernon assumed his role as the undisputed leader of the cult.

Eric Hoffer, in his thought-provoking book, *The True Believer,* could have predicted what would happen next.

"When the old order begins to crack, he [the leader prone to fanaticism] wades in with all his might and recklessness to blow the whole hated present to high heaven. He glories in the sight of a world coming to a sudden end. . . . All that already exists is rubbish, and there is no sense in reforming rubbish" (p. 131).

Vernon Howell finally took power in 1987. The world headquarters of the Branch Davidians was a scattering of rundown cottages, each no larger than a single room. But with Vernon firmly in control, the compound (and life inside) was destined for a reshaping that would change it forever.

Chapter Nine

The Seductive Seven Seals

Imagine, just for the sake of this chapter, that you are attending a sermon at Ranch Apocalypse. You are not a follower of David Koresh, at least not yet. Perhaps you found out about the young man who claims to be a prophet through a close friend, or perhaps he made a ruckus during your church service. You're wondering how people could get so excited about what he is teaching and why they willingly give up virtually everything for this man. In any case you've decided to give him a fair hearing and compare his teachings to the Bible.

You arrive at the Branch Davidian headquarters and your friend and a number of simply dressed, friendly people greet you. The children seem well-behaved, and the family-type atmosphere impresses you.

After a light supper of fruit and popcorn, you sit beside your friend on a wooden bench and wait for the man they claim is a prophet. When he arrives, you're somewhat taken aback. Instead of a three-piece suit, David Koresh sports tennis shoes and a pair of old jeans. And instead of a neatly-combed preppy haircut, he has a somewhat greasy mane of brown hair. However, those dimples just below his wire-frame glasses are somewhat charming. You decide to give him a chance.

◆◆◆

Koresh starts out with what appears to be a traditional Christian sermon. He describes the life of Christ, stressing Christ's character and blameless life. "'And ye know that he was manifested to take away our sins; and in him is no sin' (1 John 3:5)," Koresh quotes from memory.

For more than an hour he quotes texts and relates biblical stories in support of his thesis that Christ was perfect and never sinned. He finally ends with, "'For he hath made him to be sin for us, who knew no sin' (2 Cor. 5:21)."

You nod your head in agreement. After all, the majority of Christians today would agree that Christ led a sinless life. That's an accepted and orthodox Christian teaching. Come to think of it, you just read an explanation of it the other day in that book *Seventh-day Adventists Believe* . . .

But wait. Koresh is moving on. The next segment of his sermon emphasizes the incredible work done by Christ's apostles after His death. Men of power, they went about teaching and healing, often stoned and persecuted but always standing firm for their beliefs.

He quotes text after text detailing the activities of the apostles and their close connection with God. This, too, you can't dispute, although he seems to have forgotten the denials by Peter and the sometimes stormy relationship between Peter and Paul and between Paul and Barnabas.

Turning to the book of Acts, Koresh describes the scene of Pentecost. In addition to being true men of God, Christ's disciples had the Holy Spirit. "Do you have the Holy Spirit?" he asks.

You wonder. Sometimes you're not too sure, especially after just hearing of the sterling record of Christ and His followers.

Another hour has passed, and you hardly even know it. The others in the room seem totally caught up in the sermon, and it's contagious. More than anything else in the world you would like to have the Holy Spirit, to be ready for Christ's soon appearing.

You sense that Koresh may be about to tell you how.

Jumping to the book of Revelation, he describes the seven churches. He emphasizes the purity of the first church and the messages of commendation that the members received for their committed faithfulness. You wonder if you can ever measure up.

After citing the message to the church of Laodicea, Koresh points out the failings of the church today. "'Because thou art lukewarm, and neither cold nor hot, I will spue thee out of my mouth' (Rev. 3:16)," he chants, doing his best imitation of a Jonathan Edwards' sermon. And he's successful, because you're beginning to feel like a sinner in the hands of an angry God, a lukewarm Christian, and you're about to be spit out, or as the Greek says, vomited out.

Koresh quotes text after text that point to the sinfulness of human nature, namely, your sinfulness. He never mentions any verses that point to your salvation, and you're too overwhelmed to think of them. Awash in a sea of Scripture, you can only listen and hope there's hope. But he gives no hope, at least not yet.

Christ expects nothing short of perfection from each of His followers, Koresh goes on. You are bound by the command "Be ye therefore perfect, even as your Father which is in heaven is perfect" (Matt. 5:48).

The sermon has lasted four hours now, and you wish you could go to the bathroom. But no one else is moving, and before you ever sat down, your friend informed you that the prophet does not take kindly to interruptions, even for physical necessity. His is an important message, and you might miss out on some point affecting your eternal destiny. So you sit and listen, wishing Koresh will soon offer some hope of redemption. At the moment you're feeling somewhat discouraged, and that's exactly where he wants you. But wait, he's got one more nail to drive into your coffin before he offers any solution.

You realize that, like every other human, you're far from perfect. You sin and have sinned, like everyone else. "For all have sinned, and come short of the glory of God" (Rom. 3:23). Koresh hammers this point home for two to three hours, until you are destitute of any hope, exhausted, and desperate for any hint of salvation (as well as a rest room!).

Then he turns to the inspiration of the Holy Spirit behind all Scripture. For "all scripture is given by inspiration of God" (2 Tim. 3:16), he harangues, among other points.

You nod your head in agreement as he goes over and over this point, wondering what it has to do with the first part of the sermon and wishing that you could stretch your legs.

Now Koresh blasts any faint spiritual hope you may have had left. The Scripture is given by God, by His Holy Spirit. You, by sinning, have rejected the Holy Scripture, and by doing so, have sinned against the Holy Spirit!

Now Koresh rises to his full height and glares directly at you. "'Verily I say unto you,' he shouts, 'All sins shall be forgiven unto the sons of men, and blasphemies wherewith soever they shall blaspheme: but he that shall blaspheme against the Holy Ghost hath never forgiveness, but is in danger of eternal damnation' (Mark 3:28, 29)."

If you weren't so tired, so uncomfortable, and so enraptured with Koresh's endless ability to quote Scripture after Scripture, you might have thought of 1 John 2:1: "My little children, these things write I unto you, that ye sin not. And if any man sin, we have an advocate with the Father, Jesus Christ the righteous."

But all you've heard for the past six hours is the terribleness of your own condition, and you're starting to believe it. You're convinced beyond any shadow of a doubt that you're going to hell. There's no way out. Not only have you slighted the name of Christ by being less than a perfect Christian, but also you have committed the unpardonable sin by rejecting the Bible, which is what tells you that you should have been perfect!

Your eyes are droopy, you feel wilted, worth nothing, and alone. You can tell that others in the room share your deep depression. It is here, when you have sunk in a mire of messy emotions, that Koresh finally offers you some hope. The would-be prophet turns to Revelation 4 and 5, and brings your attention to the fact that all hope is not lost. The Spirit, whom you have so sinfully rejected, is still trying to tell you something. "'He that hath an ear, let him hear what the Spirit saith unto the churches' (Rev. 3:22)," Koresh intones.

Your tired ears perk up one more time. While it has been the longest sermon you've ever heard, maybe there's still hope that you'll find a resolution to this matter tonight.

(What you don't know is that six hours of preaching is only the beginning. This is vintage David Koresh, and he has only begun to speak!)

So what could the Holy Spirit possibly be trying to say, in these last days, to your poor lost soul? The message seems to be sealed in a special scroll, closed with seven seals. Unfortunately, there seems to be a problem. No one is worthy to open the book.

"'And I saw a strong angel,'" Koresh says emphatically, "'proclaiming with a loud voice, Who is worthy to open the book, and to loose the seals thereof? And no man in heaven, nor in earth, neither under the earth, was able to open the book, neither to look thereon. And I wept much, because no man was found worthy to open and to read the book, neither to look thereon' (Rev. 5:2-4)."

Like John, you feel moved to tears. Here the book containing the only hope for your eternal salvation lies right in front of your face, and you must still perish because no one is worthy to open it! Koresh hammers it home. This book is the only chance you have. If the book remains closed, you might as well go out and commit suicide, since you're doomed and lost anyway.

But wait! Just as Koresh brings you once more to the brink of despair, he points you to Revelation 5:5: "Weep not: behold the Lion of the tribe of Judah, the Root of David, hath prevailed to open the book, and to loose the seven seals thereof."

Then Koresh goes into a long exposition of Revelation 5. At this point he does not break it to you that he is the "lamb." Even in your current exhausted state, you might not be ready for that—yet.

Instead, he drums home text after text describing the lamb. Over and over he returns to two of his most important points: (1) The lamb is the only one worthy to open the book, and (2) Because the lamb can open the book, he is worthy of honor, riches, and power.

Moving on to an exposition of the meaning of the seven seals, Koresh quotes with excitement, "'And I saw when the Lamb opened one of the seals,' 'and I heard, as it were the noise of thunder, one of the four beasts saying, Come and see. And I saw, and behold a white horse: and he that sat on him had a bow; and a crown was given unto him: and he went forth conquering, and to conquer' (Rev. 6:1, 2).

"I, the prophet, am the rider on the white horse," Koresh declares.

You raise one tired eyebrow, but by now your mind is pretty much like an empty pail, and Koresh keeps pouring in his deadly mixture of Revelation theology and mind control.

"The rider on the white horse goes forth, 'conquering and to conquer,'" Koresh points out. If you could only remember that Seventh-day Adventists historically have believed that the white horse symbolizes Christianity, especially the purity of the early Christian church as it spread across the ancient world.

But to Koresh, he is the man on the white horse. He conquers by inseminating as many women as possible. Only the children of the man on the white horse are righteous, according to him. God's plan is to destroy all the wicked children and populate the earth with children of the rider on the white horse, namely David Koresh!

"'Out of the mouths of babes and sucklings hast thou ordained strength because of thine enemies,'" rambles Koresh, pulling a text from Psalm 8:2. "'For thou hast made him a little lower than the angels,'" Koresh quotes, "'and hast crowned him with glory and honour'" (verse 5).

If by this time you're feeling a little skeptical, Koresh seems to be reading your mind. He turns to Psalm 60:3: "Thou hast shewed thy people hard things: thou hast made us to drink the wine of astonishment."

Having explained the first seal to his satisfaction, Koresh turns to the second seal. "And when he had opened the second seal, I heard the second beast say, Come and see. And there went out another horse that was red: and power was given to him that sat thereon to take peace from the earth, and that they should kill one another: and there was given unto him a great sword" (Rev. 6:3, 4).

"There will be a great war centered in Israel," Koresh interprets.

That sounds like what a lot of other evangelical Christians think, you muse.

But Koresh doesn't stop there. He goes on to explain that he is also the rider on the red horse and hence will either start the war or at least be the center of its focus. You drift into your own thoughts for a moment, remembering several trips to Israel that Koresh had taken. Your friend had told you that at one point Koresh taught that he would go to Israel and get the whole ball rolling.

Koresh cites Zechariah, chapters 1 through 4, which conveniently enough speak about a red horse. He uses the chapters at length to prove that he is the Lord and also to back up his all-women-belong-to-me doctrine.

By now it is well past midnight, and you wonder how long his sermon is going to take. But you've never heard anyone expound the Bible the way this man does, with such conviction and that "look" in his eye.

Koresh turns to the third seal. "And when he had opened the third seal, I heard the third beast say, Come and see. And I beheld, and lo a black horse; and he that sat on him had a pair of balances in His hand. And I heard a voice in the midst of the four beasts say, A measure of wheat for a penny, and three measures of barley for a penny; and see thou hurt not the oil and the wine" (Rev. 6:5, 6).

God is the rider on the black horse, Koresh contends. And God has the balances in His hand. He quotes Hosea 12:7, "He is a merchant, the balances of deceit are in his hand: he loveth to oppress," and then draws a dangerous conclusion. "God loves to deceive people!" God can lie, cheat, or do whatever simply by claiming that it is necessary for the person's salvation!

If you were to study this passage in its context, you would understand that Hosea is actually condemning those who falsify weights and measures to make a profit, namely the northern kingdom of Israel. But since you're not a walking Bible commentary, for the moment you can't argue with his interpretation.

Koresh ties in passages in the books of Ezekiel, Psalms, Revelation, and Zechariah, in with the black horse to develop a detailed world government conspiracy theory.

The United Nations, the Roman Catholic Church, the Seventh-day Adventists, the United States government, and the "merchants of the earth" are all privy to this plan, which revolves around the economy.

You can hardly hold your head up for exhaustion by the time Howell gets to the fourth seal. "And when he had opened the fourth seal, I heard the voice of the fourth beast say, Come and see. And I looked, and behold a pale horse: and his name that sat on him was Death, and Hell followed with him. And power was given unto them over the fourth part of the earth, to kill with sword, and with hunger, and with death, and with the beasts of the earth" (Rev. 6:7, 8).

Once again, Koresh identifies himself as the rider on the horse. He uses the text to justify his killing of his enemies, which can take place either before or after the establishment of God's earthly kingdom.

You remember hearing of the Branch Davidians' prediction of a 1959 "divine slaughter" of Seventh-day Adventists and wonder if Koresh feels that it's his mission to fulfill the "prophecy" as he sees fit.

Quoting text after text after text to support his views on the fourth seal, Koresh goes on at length from the books of Ezekiel and Zechariah. Finally he winds up that seal with a vivid description of the Israelites slaying the ungodly in the Old Testament.

With that in mind you're ready for the opening of the fifth seal. "And when he had opened the fifth seal, I saw under the altar the souls of them that were slain for the word of God, and for the testimony which they held: and they cried with a loud voice, saying, How long, O Lord, holy and true, dost thou not judge and avenge our blood on them that dwell on the earth? And white robes were given unto every one of them; and it was said unto them, that they should rest yet for a little season, until their fellowservants also and their brethren, that should be killed as they were, should be fulfilled" (Rev. 6:9-11).

"Throughout history, 200 million martyrs will give their lives for Christ before the number is fulfilled," Koresh states.

You had been nodding off, but that one jerks you awake in shock. How'd he get that number?

As if reading your mind, Koresh summarily cites Revelation 9:15, 16: "And the four angels were loosed, which were prepared for an hour, and a day, and a month, and a year, for to slay the third part of men. And the number of the army of the horsemen were two hundred thousand thousand: and I heard the number of them."

In order to fulfill this number, Koresh claims, all his followers must die. However, a few (among them, conveniently, himself) will not see death, but will be translated. Those of his followers who die will help make up the number of the 200 million, which already includes all the martyrs of the Dark Ages until modern times.

Koresh explains that God will not come and set up His kingdom until the full number of martyrs has been reached. "Since God has not come yet," Koresh maintains, "the number of martyrs is not yet complete." And since the rest of the world is Babylon (worshiping the dragon of Revelation 13), the Branch Davidians represent the only true informed body of believers on earth. Branch Davidians, then, are the only ones who could qualify as martyrs for Christ! And Koresh employs a vast array of Scripture to support his belief. He quotes from Isaiah, the Psalms, Revelation, Daniel, Zechariah, and 2 Thessalonians to support his interpretation of this seal and to show that his followers must suffer and die for him.

You were nodding off again, but after this "revelation" suddenly you are wide awake. This man is telling you that if you want eternal life, you must give up everything and die for him.

Koresh moves on to the sixth seal, which shows the coming of the Lord and the setting up of His kingdom. "I am the lamb," he drawls in his soft voice. Then he rattles off texts from Ezekiel, the Psalms, Isaiah, Joel, Matthew, Mark, Luke, and 1 Thessalonians to drive home his points. The sixth seal says that the lamb comes down, which is why Koresh maintains he will be translated before he can come again!

You shake your head. This is unlike anything you've ever heard before!

Finally Koresh reaches the seventh and last seal. Boggled, you hope that his sermon will soon end so that maybe you can clear the cobwebs out of your head and think it through.

What you don't know is that, to Koresh, the seventh seal extends from Revelation chapter 8 through the end of the book! And you're in for it!

Koresh spends the next few hours expounding on the seven trumpets, the woman of Revelation 12, the beast of Revelation 13, and the messages of God in Revelation 14. Then he moves on to the seven last plagues in Revelation 15 and 16, a discussion of Babylon as found in Revelation 17-19, and the thousand-year period of chapter 20.

When he starts discussing the final destruction of the wicked and the new heavens and the earth, you breathe a sigh of relief. This was interesting, but you're into the wee hours of the morning and can't wait to use the bathroom and get some sleep.

But Koresh is not through with you yet. He goes back and,

just for your doubting mind, drives home his final and crowning points one more time.

"Only the lamb can open the seals and reveal their meaning," Koresh says. "During the past 15 hours, I, Koresh, have opened the meaning of those seals to you as you have never heard them before. Therefore, I, Koresh, must be the lamb!

"And because I, Koresh, am the lamb, I am worthy of honor, riches, praise, and power. I am the only one worthy on heaven and earth! I am the only one entitled to anything in heaven or on earth! I own everyone and everything! I own you, and only through me can you achieve salvation."

With that, Koresh finishes his sermon and sits down.

◆◆◆

When the resident prophet finally finishes his sermon at 5:00 a.m., your legs are numb, your backside is sore, and you might have wet your pants a long time ago. But your mind is reeling with the incredible array of Scripture drilled into your head. Could he really be the prophet?

Suddenly his grimy fingernails and greasy hair don't seem quite so repulsive. After all, Christ was a carpenter. And David Koresh just might have the light. This man knows his Bible like no one you've ever seen!

Confused, you stumble to your bed in the back of a retired school bus. On the way out you notice one of the Mighty Men tapping a young (and also exhausted) girl on the shoulder. While you catch a few hours of sleep, the prophet, who sleeps until 2:00 p.m. each day, wants to exercise his "ownership of all heaven and earth" over the unfortunate young woman.

If you were Lonnie Little, a longtime Seventh-day Adventist church member who was simply trying to free his son from this madness, you might just be lucky enough to get yourself out of there posthaste.

But be prepared. Lonnie said that it took him two years to get his head screwed on straight again after a two-day visit to Ranch Apocalypse.

If you were Sherri Jewell, you'd call your mother and say, "He's teaching us so much!"

If you were Marc Breault or Steve Schneider, you'd be incredulous at first but interested enough to keep listening. And if you were Steve Schneider, that would be your downfall.

But whoever you are, if someone ever sits you down for a 15-hour sermon or anything like it, pounds over the same set of lopsided texts again and again, and keeps you sitting until your back aches, your bladder bursts, and your legs couldn't straighten if they had to, remember this: You better stretch those legs, relieve that bladder, and find some reason to stay in the bathroom for a long, long time.

Because what David Koresh did was not preaching. It was brainwashing!

Chapter Ten

❖

Little Women in Waiting

It's in the Bible. King David was getting old, feeble, and probably a little crotchety. Worse than that, he was cold and just couldn't get warmed up. Especially at night. His feet felt frosty, his cheeks were chilly, his hands were hostile to heat. Why Bathsheba couldn't help him, we're not told. Maybe she was old and cold too!

In any case, the king's true and trusty advisers were not long in finding a solution. Abishag. She was young. She was beautiful. And, best of all, she was warm.

Enter another David, nearly 3,000 years later. Add an uncanny knack for finding convenient biblical models for whatever behavior he wanted to emulate. Stir in a devout following who believed that he was a prophet and worshiped his every step. And there you have it—the recipe for a new tradition at Ranch Apocalypse, described in Marc Breault's book *Inside the Cult,* and aptly named "abishag."

David Koresh was young, something less than feeble, and probably not cold. But abishag, the practice of taking young girls to bed with him to "warm him up" as a prelude to later activities, became an accepted routine at Ranch Apocalypse, according to Breault.

◆◆◆

"Thou shalt not commit adultery." So reads the seventh commandment, and it applies to everyone. Unless you're David Koresh, the sinful messiah. You make the rules. You interpret Scripture to justify whatever pleases you. And you may even claim to have a vision in which God commands you "to give seed to many women."

Incredibly, David Koresh's followers bought into the concept, as they also did his other strange ideas. Captivated by his leadership, they blindly allowed him to take any woman in the cult he wanted—married or unmarried, young or old.

To justify his actions, Koresh cited Bible heroes such as Abraham, David, Solomon, and others who practiced polygamy. Conveniently, he forgot to note the trouble that could accrue from this form of family. And David Koresh's practice of abishag was, technically speaking, not the same as biblical polygamy.

Polygamy involves the socially sanctioned concept of taking more than one legal wife. God, through Moses, even regulated the practice, especially the rights of the additional wives (Ex. 21:10; Lev. 18:18; Deut. 21:15-17). Polygamy involved no divorce or remarriage. It did not allow taking any woman one might desire as a sexual partner. In Scripture it is not considered a violation of the commandment prohibiting adultery. That does not mean, however, that polygamy went without critique. Deuteronomy 17:17 warns Israelite kings against multiplying wives—as well as silver and gold.

Adultery and fornication, on the other hand, Scripture refused to accept. It roundly condemned sexual profligacy, as well it should.

So in his 15-hour Bible studies, which began around 3:00 p.m. and continued through the night, Koresh found plenty of uncondemned examples of polygamy by which he bewildered his followers with a perplexing array of texts from various biblical books, and then intertwined quotations from Ellen White, mixing a small bit of truth with his own peculiar ideas. He did not enlighten them as to the distinction in Scripture between polygamy, adultery, and fornication.

The following statement, from the book *Inside the Cult,* by Marc Breault, gives just a small sampling of the rambling style that became Vernon's trademark: "The people of the world, Christianity, worship the Bible. They idolize these men who lived 2,000-3,000 years ago. Yet look at the Bible. Look at what it's saying. Abraham had more than one wife. David had more than one wife. Solomon had a thousand. Can you imagine taking a thousand wives down to McDonald's? How much would that have cost him? Yet these stupid Christians, with their stupid scholars, will condemn me one day for having more than one wife. They don't even know the [one word deleted] book they say they believe" (p. 73).

Because the compound residents ate sporadically, worked long hours at various chores, and often went without sleep to hear Koresh's all-night sermons, they were especially vulnerable to his teachings. And his sermons did nothing more than reinforce his role as absolute, no-questions-asked leader.

His sermons, although sprinkled with quotations from Ellen White, did not, however, include information about what she thought about polygamy, fornication, and adultery. "Hundreds of years before Solomon came to the throne, the Lord, foreseeing the perils that would beset those who might be chosen as rulers of Israel, gave Moses instruction for their guidance. . . . In connection with this instruction the Lord particularly cautioned the one who might be anointed king not to 'multiply wives to himself, that his heart turn not away'" *(Prophets and Kings,* p. 52). And it is hardly the only place where Ellen White addressed the bane of polygamy!

David Koresh disregarded the teaching of Scripture on the sacredness of marriage and the family. Being deeply in love with himself, he stopped at nothing to build his "holy harem" of girls and women whom he never legally married, but who remained legally single or the lawfully wedded wife of another husband.

◆◆◆

It all began in 1983 when his love affair with the 70-year-old Lois Roden hit the skids. Perhaps Vernon was just tired of her. In any case, he suddenly announced, "God commanded me to marry Rachel."

Rachel's parents, cult members Perry and Mary Bell Jones, readily agreed to the marriage of their 14-year-old daughter to the up-and-coming Davidian leader, Vernon Howell.

The blonde-haired beauty subsequently bore him two children, of which Cyrus was reputed to be his favorite. But Rachel's attractiveness didn't keep Vernon's eyes at home. Soon he took as his second "wife" the slightly built Karen Doyle, daughter of another cult member and also just 14 years old.

Vernon now had two 14-year-old sex partners. Marc Breault explained in *Inside the Cult:* "In Rachel's case, she was legally married to Vernon. This allowed him to portray himself as a devoted family man. But in Karen's case, and it was to be the same in all future conquests, there was no formal wedding ceremony. And this suited Vernon just fine, because then he could dump his women, or girls, as it pleased him, with no legal repercussions" (p. 62).

When Karen's father heard about the union, he went through the roof. But Vernon soon explained that he'd had a vision in which God had instructed him to "take Karen."

And how did Karen react? "From childhood up, this quiet, shy girl had been brought up to worship the man who was now stealing her childhood," wrote Marc Breault. "She had been taught that whatever this man said was gospel and must be obeyed" (*ibid.*, p. 63).

Rachel, in the meantime, had been banished to California, where she reportedly had a dream commanding Vernon to take even more wives. She immediately telephoned her husband to relay the message, which only confirmed and reinforced his delusion of divinity. After the dream, he felt more affirmed than ever in his practice of fornication and adultery.

Within a few short years he added as many as 18 women to his "House of David," later known as the "brides of Christ." Some were only 12 years old!

◆◆◆

Branch Davidian women subsequently left a trail of birth certificates listing no father. It was an unspoken understanding, of course, that Koresh had fathered the child. However, he feared that his name on the certificate would alert the government authorities. He had a financial reason, too, for the practice. Most of the "brides of Christ" were collecting food stamps and possibly welfare money as well.

Koresh taught that children fathered by him would one day rule the earth with him—after he and his male followers annihilated all unbelievers. With this theology as part of the Davidian mind-set, it's no wonder that they stockpiled weapons and ammunition.

Koresh's teaching became more and more outrageous, mind-boggling, and confusing. For example, he reminded his followers that he was the lamb mentioned in the Bible who would lead them to salvation. Although it wasn't a new truth to the Davidians, they weren't prepared for what followed.

He then "annulled" all marriages and claimed that all women (at least those among the Davidians) belonged to him. And the Davidian men, conveniently, were to remain celibate. "In heaven you'll get a perfect mate," David told them—apparently that was to be some sort of consolation prize!

His radical new teaching caused a major rift and jeopardized the entire Davidian organization. Eric Hoffer in *The True Believer* described the restless desire for change often exhibited in leaders of mass movements and the cost of those desires to the organization.

"The danger of the fanatic to the development of a movement

is that he cannot settle down. Once victory has been won and the new order begins to crystallize, the fanatic becomes an element of strain and disruption. The taste for strong feeling drives him on to search for mysteries yet to be revealed and secret doors yet to be opened. He keeps groping for extremes" (p. 133).

◆◆◆

The order to annul all marriages left the Davidian men numb. "Guys were in tears about it, that God wanted them to give up their wives," said a former cult member. "They were heartbroken."

Yet most stayed in the cult, and those men and women who remained quickly separated. The men crammed into dormitory-style rooms, sleeping in bunk beds nailed to the wall. The women resided in an upstairs room near the children. Eventually, the men and women came together only for Bible studies.

But when people's minds are controlled, they follow orders! Because what they are called to give up is a test of faith, they ask no questions of their fearless leader.

As one would expect in such a situation, problems arose. Marc Breault reports an outbreak of a sexually transmitted disease among Koresh's "wives," as well as jealousy and dissension.

Cult members became suspicious of one another and of the outside world. Interestingly enough, shared suspicion often serves as a unifying agent for mass movements. Awareness of their own blemishes and shortcomings often encourages people to detect ill will and meanness in others.

"Thus when the frustrated congregate in a mass movement, the air is heavy-laden with suspicion," wrote Eric Hoffer. "There is prying and spying, tense watching and a tense awareness of being watched. . . . Knowing themselves continually watched, the faithful strive to escape suspicion by adhering zealously to prescribed behavior and opinion" *(The True Believer,* p. 114).

The generous numbers of Koresh's sexual partners and the

power struggles between them kept each one vying for a better position among the "brides of Christ" and encouraged exactly the type of suspicion that often helps leaders such as Koresh retain their power.

"Fear of one's neighbors, one's friends, and even one's relatives seems to be the rule within all mass movements," continued Hoffer. "Now and then innocent people are deliberately accused and sacrificed in order to keep suspicion alive" *(ibid.,* p. 115).

One example of this might be the family with French fries' containers left over from a trip to town. Koresh promptly kicked them out of the compound.

When David Koresh took the wives of the men around him to be part of the House of David, he may have cited the example of King David taking Bathsheba from Uriah the Hittite. But the Bible also speaks clearly of the punishment and subsequent trials King David suffered.

Koresh claimed to have many "wives," but his version of multiple "marriages" seemed more like sleeping around than polygamy, because of the casual way in which he entered into his arrangements. Many of the women were still married to other men, and only Rachel was ever legally married to him.

◆◆◆

His promise of a perfect kingdom never did materialize. In fact, just the opposite occurred. Some of his most loyal supporters, including his top lieutenant, Steve Schneider, began having second thoughts regarding his "divinity." Steve Schneider was especially distressed over the treatment of the women and the harsh abuse and neglect of the children. And Marc Breault, Koresh's right-hand man, left the cult over Koresh's attempt to take his wife, Elizabeth.

Chapter Eleven

The Australian Connection

Vernon Howell was on a roll. His recruiting success in America had convinced him that he could succeed as a self-proclaimed prophet. Now the battle for the hearts and minds of the Branch Davidians moved from the land of the free and the brave to Australia.

The way of life "down under" is a unique blend of America and Britain, and the people there are made of stern stuff. Although the country's prosperity and political stability tend to mask the toughening influence of their violent early history, the heritage of the Australian has made him or her spirited, undaunted, and unafraid of the challenges on every hand. This people, with a love of sunlight, movement, and space, are highly secular. Yet they take seriously their politics, sports, and religion (when they are religious). They are willing to battle for what they believe.

Into this vigorous and impressive culture stepped the scruffy, unkempt Howell. Traveling by jumbo jet, he arrived in Melbourne in February of 1986. Wearing a cheap suit, he carried his expensive guitar in one hand and a study Bible in the other. He came as a charismatic, beer-swilling, self-proclaimed Christ and self-proclaimed son of the Holy Spirit.

The fact that an element of the Branch Davidians already existed in Australia aided his recruitment drive. The Davidians, more widely known as the Shepherd's Rod, were a significant force in Australia in the 1960s and 1970s, causing much dissension and turmoil for Adventists during that time. However, when Vernon came to Australia, the Davidian influence had greatly diminished. And his "spies"—cult members who quietly infiltrated church groups—had done their advance surveillance and felt that there was potential for membership growth.

Although Howell traveled with Clive Doyle, a former Australian—now an American citizen—he didn't impress the local Davidian group at first. Those assembled to take a look at this new prophet had many initial misgivings.

For one thing, anti-Vernon literature came on a regular basis to the Australian Davidians from George Roden. People were skeptical, and Vernon understood quite well that it was crucial for him to recruit . . . and also calm! He hoped to overturn the negative impression that the Australians already had of him.

Also he wanted desperately to win them to his side in his quest to wrench power from George Roden.

But the group he lectured to that first evening couldn't understand his philosophy. His rambling, often incoherent, lecture of several hours left them confused and disgusted.

"We couldn't understand his point. We couldn't find his point even after all those hours of listening to him," said Lisa Gent, who later joined the cult with her husband and children.

Vernon perceived their lack of interest and moved into another method of manipulation—scare tactics. He threatened the group with eternal loss if they didn't go to Palestine, Texas, for the Passover that year.

One couple who ultimately found his devout theology attractive was Bruce and Lisa Gent, a talented twosome who desperately wanted to follow God's will. Bruce, a builder, and Lisa, a musician, maintained a classy lifestyle in a lovely home with a swimming pool.

Vernon chastised them for their materialistic lifestyle, and they secretly wondered if he might be right. They thought that perhaps they did spend too much money on themselves and that maybe they should be more concerned with those less fortunate. After all, here was someone preaching simplicity and sacrifice—certainly rare in their secular culture.

◆◆◆

In an article written by Bruce Manners, editor of the South Pacific Division *Record,* he tells of the reaction of others who heard Vernon.

A former member of the Branch Davidians, now an Adventist, said, "When I first came in contact with Vernon Howell, he was reasonable and well-read as far as Scriptures are concerned, but then so is the devil. He was a tool of the devil if ever there was one.

"He started in a gentle, pleasant manner. He spoke about how he was going to right wrongs in the world. He had a message to spread. He wanted to rid the world of its ills and hurts."

It is difficult to impress Australians, but somehow Vernon eventually managed to do just that. In his relations with this breezy, unpredictable people, he found himself passing through three stages: First, he encountered skepticism. Second, when he touched on some raw and secret nerve, they viewed him with a baleful eye. But by the third, he managed to win the Australians over by his constant preaching. Again, his incredible knowledge of Scripture and his ability to disarm and confuse convinced the group that if they did not accept his message they were headed straight to hell!

Soon some of them were hooked. For others his word slowly became the word of God. Because their theological background already included a prophetic message, they couldn't be sure that this man claiming to be a modern-day messiah really wasn't what he said he was.

The most significant factor to their acceptance of his message was that they were already advent believers. They seemed somehow predisposed to the hysteria of a Second Coming—harboring a final persecution complex. Their mind-set dwelt on the negatives of the future—turmoil—the militant theology. It would seem that they were not that rooted and grounded in Scripture themselves! Although they were certainly not misfits, they seem to have had a lack of basic biblical understanding.

Another former member of the Branch Davidians, who is also now a Seventh-day Adventist, said, "Vernon was a very dangerous man. He convinced us that what he said was right. When anyone comes who claims to have new light, we should face it, not hide it. In particular, we should not hide it from our young people. We should be very open. We've got nothing to lose by this, and we've got nothing to hide. The best thing we can do is to get our own act together and become genuine. Maybe that's the hardest thing for us to do."

◆◆◆

When Vernon started to recruit in Melbourne, it was hard for Pastor Barry Whelan to cope with the charismatic imposter. But cope he did—in the only way he knew how—by "calling sin by its right name."

Again we quote from a *Record* article written by Bruce Manners. In it Pastor Whelan discusses Vernon's activities in his church.

"This was probably the most traumatic time in my ministry. We lost some of our youth to this guy. He used well-trained followers—people he had taken and trained—and they moved into our youth Sabbath school. They targeted new members and any who had some dissatisfaction with the church.

"They told them that he had new light that they ought to hear. And they arranged to meet them at night. Then Howell used what I would call brainwashing techniques for 10-12 hours solid to get these people hooked.

"Vernon Howell was such an intense fellow—the kind of person who would stare you out. He was charismatic. He was shrewd. At first he appeared to be on the side of the church, but then he began to create doubts about the ministry and then the church.

"The people he affected were like my own children. I'd studied the Bible with them. I'd baptized them, and I'd even married one couple."

Pastor Whelan recalls attending a meeting with another pastor, Pawel Cieslar, and being surprised to find about 20 of his church members present. A new follower had rung the members, inviting them to this meeting, and implied that they were needed because their pastor would be unable to attend.

"I walked into that place and had an immediate sense of coldness. I remember saying to Pawel, 'I don't want to be in this place.' It had that kind of feel about it.

"We stayed until he implied that he was Jesus. At that point I said to him, 'That's enough.' I stood and walked out, and many of the folk there followed me. Howell shouted at us, 'I threw them out of my Father's house 2,000 years ago, and now I throw you Pharisees out.'

"I remember one of the girls on the lawn in front of the house saying, 'But pastor, he's Jesus! He's Jesus!'"

Pastor Whelan received a death threat after this encounter, and we have not used the names of individuals interviewed for this story because of threats of violence against those who have any connections with the Branch Davidians.

◆◆◆

Perhaps the thing that saved some of Howell's potential victims was that they stayed in Australia while others followed him to America.

"After Vernon left Australia and the people had time to think, they realized their error," Bruce Manners told us on the telephone.

Graeme Craddock, an Australian who was in the compound during the fire, escaped with minor burns and shock. His parents told Bruce Manners that they didn't know he was becoming involved until he had fully committed himself to the sect. They said, "He was a keen Bible student and very involved in church. But as this came on he began to withdraw himself. He would tend to stay at home rather than go to church. He seemed to be of the opinion that people at church were talking their own philosophies and wouldn't listen to sound instruction."

They also said that he deceived them regarding his whereabouts and that they had discovered they could do nothing to change his mind. They felt extremely frustrated at not being able to pinpoint a reason why he joined the cult. "If we're looking for things as a warning to others, maybe we're going about it the wrong way, because we may not recognize the next false track that is going to be laid down," they observed.

"It is not our wisdom that is going to uncover it: It is going to be our connection with God. Those who are truly being led by the Spirit will pick the warning signs because one of the gifts of the Spirit is to be able to discern these things."

June Craddock commented that she felt they were in spiritual warfare. "We had to take hold of the divine," she said. "I got down on my knees and said, 'Lord, I don't understand it. Just give me peace.' And the Lord gave me the peace He has promised."

Mr. and Mrs. Craddock were extremely fortunate that their son survived. Their faith in God and their prayers have been rewarded, and yet other parents prayed also. Why weren't their children saved?

Could it be that this predisposition to cultism had its seeds in the growing-up years? Could it be that those who were deceived relied too heavily on someone else's thinking, thus playing into the hands of an imposter?

God alone knows the answers to these questions. And without Him none of us is safe from false teaching.

As a result of Howell's recruiting in Australia, seven Australians were inside the Waco compound. During the standoff only one escaped death.

CHAPTER TWELVE

HONOLULU GOLD MINE

Vernon Howell, a.k.a. David Koresh, needed help. With the beginnings of his holy harem of the brides of Christ now in place, his goal was to build up an army of followers.

He turned for help to the smooth-talking Marc Breault, recruited in a Loma Linda supermarket by cult member Perry Jones.

Disillusioned with the church and searching for meaning and a purpose in his life, Marc found the Branch Davidians to be friendly, intense, and a group with a strong sense of mission. But the most powerful pull of all was the Davidian zeal to enfold him with their philosophy. In reality, David needed his expertise. Marc's ability to talk, his sensitive and caring nature, and his love of music and computers fit right in with Koresh's need for a top-ranking lieutenant. Soon Marc was Vernon's right-hand man and top recruiter.

In seeking followers, Marc realized the potential gold mine in his home state of Hawaii. In Hawaii he knew people, and there was money to be tapped.

In June of 1986 Marc flew to Hawaii to recruit some of his old friends from the Diamond Head Seventh-day Adventist Church.

◆◆◆

The recent addition of numerous young adults to the Diamond Head congregation had brought an infusion of enthusiasm and life to the conservative church. The older members adored the young people—a potpourri of class and culture. Vibrant and like a breath of fresh air, the new converts and those who had recently moved to Hawaii, like Sherri Jewell and Jeff Little, swept themselves into the hearts and lives of not only the church members but also of the pastor, Max Torkelsen II.

A young man of 35 at the time, Pastor Torkelsen threw himself into his church work with dedication and fervor. He loved his job, his church, and his congregation.

"I felt such a sense of excitement, because of the miracles God had done in bringing new members to the church," Pastor Torkelsen remarked later. "We had a newly remodeled sanctuary, and our congregation was totally supportive of the young adults, many of whom were converts."

Unfortunately, trouble lay ahead for members of the loving and growing Diamond Head church. And in a million years they'd never have predicted how successful Vernon Howell would be when he arrived in Hawaii soon after Breault.

Pastor Torkelsen recalls vividly the first time he laid eyes on Vernon Howell. "One Sabbath as I was greeting church members, I glanced over the arriving congregation and was startled to observe a man with long greasy hair and dressed in a flowing white robe. The robe was cinched around the middle with a piece of frayed rope."

"As I moved toward him and extended my hand," Pastor Torkelsen later explained, "his piercing eyes bore through me as he introduced himself. 'I'm Vernon Jezreel from California,' he said," in a tone Pastor Torkelsen took for haughty piety.

Getting his foot in the door of the church proved to be easy for Vernon with Marc as his front man. Marc's best friend in school had been Steve Schneider, himself a bit disgruntled with the Adventist Church because he had not received a call to the ministry.

After church the first Sabbath that Vernon was in Hawaii Marc introduced him around, and young people immediately surrounded Vernon.

"Jezreel's" amazing knowledge of Scripture, bewildering fluency, and charismatic personality captivated the young adults. They quickly sought permission to hold Bible studies in the church.

"Mental alarm bells were already sounding a caution warning as I responded," Pastor Torkelsen said, recalling the request. "I don't feel comfortable with you studying in the church," the pastor told the church members.

"Since I felt personally responsible for what happened in the church, I could not grant permission for him to teach a class until I had opportunity to know more about him," Pastor Torkelsen later commented.

The pastor also recalls that Mr. Jezreel, as Howell called himself then, spoke with authority and indignation when Torkelsen refused to open the church. "This is my Father's house, and I have a right to teach here," he claimed.

Pastor Torkelsen did not at that time understand the implication of the "sinful messiah's" statement. However, he does recall that the young adult church members considered their pastor rude and unreasonable at the time. So, going against the advice of their pastor, the group organized a Bible study class anyway—in a member's home.

"The studies lasted into the wee hours of the morning, night after night," Torkelsen recalls.

Because the majority of those in the group worked or attended classes, they'd stay up most of the night. And in their sleep-deprived condition it became virtually impossible for them to adequately discern truth from error.

"The length and intensity of the studies lent an aura of deep spirituality, which proved very appealing, albeit intemperate," Pastor Torkelsen said.

Vernon's mesmerizing effect on those around him seemed to fuel a seductive and bewitching pull. And his amazing ability to quote huge portions of Scripture and his confident air of authority totally captivated the 30 or so young adults, many of whom had money and influence.

Vernon's bewitched followers received little chance to comment or disagree with his theology. In the new scheme of things, only Vernon's interpretation and agenda mattered.

Howell must have realized what was at stake in this Hawaiian paradise, because he gave his all. He typed letters, handed and mailed them out, and worked feverishly to form the new nucleus for his cult. And his innocent, loving group of listeners, despite their diverse wealth of expertise, education, and money, totally fell for him.

His teaching of a major earthquake to hit the West Coast particularly caught their attention. "He urged everyone to join him in warning the sinful state of California. He proposed forming a rock band and touring the state, evangelizing the world for Vernon Jezreel," Torkelsen said.

Vernon's invasion of the Diamond Head Seventh-day Adventist Church had only begun when Max Torkelsen transferred to another congregation. For several months the church went without a pastor, and it was during this time Howell moved in with a mighty wave.

His efforts intensified, and he continued the lengthy Bible studies. Soon the church board felt that they must deal with this mysterious man. And yet it was with a great deal of pain that they reached their conclusion. They loved and deeply cared for the young people of their congregation. And they had a deep commitment that any dealings should reflect only compassion and great patience.

The board finally called a church business meeting, and it was there that Vernon Howell publicly declared his claims to be the "Messiah."

That was the sign the church board had been waiting for. They now knew him to be an imposter. A brokenhearted constituency realized that there could be no reconciliation with this philosophy. That night the Diamond Head church disfellowshipped 12 members, including Jeff Little, Sherri Jewell, and Steve and Judy Schneider.

In the years following, Pastor Torkelsen kept in contact with his former friends and constantly prayed for them. "They were wonderful people," he said. "Not strange. They did not have, to my knowledge, tendencies toward fanaticism. They were lured with promises and by a strange attraction. They started out believing they were in revival."

◆◆◆

Long after the group left Hawaii, moving first to California and then to Waco, church members agonized over what they could have done to prevent their friends from being disfellowshipped. Some of the hard lessons that Hawaiian members say they learned were:

- New members need close monitoring and spiritual mentoring for several years after baptism.
- Converts need a sense of mission, especially the young and idealistic.
- Continuing in-depth Bible study for a new member is a must.
- Those who harbor personal animosity against the organized church need immediate and personal attention.
- Those who tend to follow self-proclaimed messiahs have had similar personality characteristics, in that they seek guidance in the most mundane areas of their lives.

◆◆◆

We must remember, of course, that numerous young people did *not* choose to follow Vernon Howell. He repulsed many, and they refused to be drawn by his tactics.

For those personal friends and family members who lost loved ones in the Waco fire, it might be well to remember that "Christ will lead His redeemed ones beside the river of life and will explain to them all that perplexed them in this world. The mysteries of grace will unfold before them. Where their finite minds discerned only confusion and broken purposes, they will see the most perfect and beautiful harmony" *(Testimonies for the Church,* vol. 9, p. 194).

CHAPTER THIRTEEN

NIXED AT NEWBOLD?

During the summer of 1988 Steve Schneider set out for Britain to repeat on the campus of Newbold College the success that Vernon Howell had already experienced in Hawaii.

According to *Inside the Cult,* Schneider arrived in London armed with nothing more than a Bible, a duffel bag, and his own silver tongue.

Unlike the Diamond Head Seventh-day Adventist Church, which had been without a pastor during part of the recruitment drive, church leaders at Newbold were aware of Schneider's presence and took immediate steps to offset his efforts.

At first they believed that the efforts at Newbold to defeat the Davidians had been quite successful, but later evidence proved that the message had spread to more than originally estimated. According to a statement from the British Union Conference: "Newbold gave Schneider no quarter, though he found off-campus opportunities to talk to small groups of students. A senior member of Newbold's staff, Dr. Hugh Dunton, monitored the activities of Schneider and sounded the necessary warnings in the appropriate quarters. Hence when Vernon Howell arrived at Bracknell in the summer, all measures were taken by the college authorities to deny him access to students.

"Nevertheless, a church member made his or her bungalow available to Howell. Among those who went to hear him speak were Newbold students. His methods were similar to the brainwashing techniques perfected by the totalitarian regimes in the 1930s. He would speak in a monotone, without interruptions, from 9:00 a.m. until after midnight.

"A small group of students became followers. Returning to their home churches—among them, Nottingham, Derby, and Manchester—these students sought to involve their families and others. In the intervening period a number of them had moved to the Waco commune, causing tremendous heartache at home. When this issue of *Messenger* was printed it was believed that only eight were involved. Now it is clear that there were more than 20."

Shortly after his arrival in England, Schneider appeared unannounced in the men's dormitory at Newbold. Since he had no money and no place to stay, which apparently was part of the plan, some unsuspecting individuals at the college took him under their wing. He immediately began working on one of the students who proved the entering wedge in converting the whole family of Samuel Henry, with the exception of Mr. Henry himself. Samuel Henry's children left him one by one to move to Ranch Apocalypse. Finally, his wife left and joined her children also.

◆◆◆

After the shoot-out and final inferno, media attention on the Adventist Church in Britain was intense. At the peak of the crisis the British Union Conference switchboard handled more than 200 calls in one day. As a result, Adventist leaders gave three television interviews, as well as many live radio shows and countless newspaper interviews.

The British Union Conference of Seventh-day Adventists sent out a press release to the 100 British broadcasting stations, stating that the Seventh-day Adventist Church had no connection to the Branch Davidians. The same press release and a follow-up press release went to all national newspapers.

Despite efforts by the Adventist Church to distance itself from the Davidians, some of our churches in Britain actually had windows broken by angry citizens. One Adventist church member received a half brick through his living room window. Irate people insulted or assaulted other church members in the street at their places of work.

Other denominations, in some cases, were supportive. Messages backing the Seventh-day Adventist Church rolled in from the Baptist churches in Nottingham and from John Reardon, president of Council of Churches in Britain and Ireland.

British Seventh-day Adventists reacted with shock and horror to the death of their former fellow believers and the extensive and sometimes damaging media coverage associated with the whole fiasco.

Editor David Marshall, returning from a "fortnight away from the office," reported that his desk was "wilting under the weight of Waco." In an excerpt from an editorial addressed to the Adventist Church in Britain, Marshall summarized some of the lessons British Adventists suggested that their church should learn from Waco.

It's important to note here that what he has to say reflects the sentiment of many letters received on the topic, not an official statement by the British Union Conference. These suggestions may not even reflect the opinions of David Marshall himself or in some cases the authors of this book, but they do serve as food for thought:

• "that we should baptize only those who have a thorough grasp of doctrines;

• "that church discipline be used against the 'wolves that spoil the flock,' individuals whose purpose is to seduce church members away from their commitment to the faith and toward the tithe-financed, independently led groups that are, for practical purposes, separate denominations;

• "that it be understood that there are other quasicommune-type setups in different parts of the U.S.A.;

• "that the denomination—from the GC to the local conference—make clear its attitude to the independent ministry offshoots, being specific 'and not speaking in parables';

• "that the local congregations be encouraged to turn to advantage the fact that everyone has now heard of Seventh-day Adventists by a saturation of *A Quick Look at Adventists* and other denominational literature;

• "that, since the mass media clearly held the church responsible for the activities of 'fanatical fringe groups,' every attempt should be made to disassociate ourselves from such groups before another Waco occurs, perhaps in Britain;

• "that the use of pulpits be guarded more carefully than heretofore and that individual Adventists have recourse to their pastors before allowing strangers to hold meetings in their homes;

• "that, given that infiltrators and offshoots peddling 'a different gospel—which is really no gospel at all' (Gal. 1:6, 7, NIV) have been present throughout Christian history, there be a new and more powerful emphasis on 'Justification by Faith . . . the Third Angel's Message in verity' and that the British Union Conference organize Bible conferences in different parts of the union to promote a renewed study of Romans and Galatians—the invariable preparation for revival;

• "that a study be made of the methods used by Koresh, Fagan, McBean, and Sellors to draw followers from Adventism to the ideology of Waco, with which Adventism has nothing in common;

• "that Christ and Him crucified be put up front in our approach to the world, and that evidence of new birth—not a detailed grasp of prophetic interpretation, be made the first condition of membership of the Seventh-day Adventist Church."

It is interesting to note the repeated references to independent ministries whose work might be to harm or oppose rather than build up the Seventh-day Adventist Church. The British church publication actually named one large independent ministry currently at odds with the Seventh-day Adventist Church and reported that the union president has discovered a large crossover between that organization and the Branch Davidians.

Six of the 10 suggestions from British members mentioned such issues as dealing with "wolves that spoil the flock," other quasicommune-type setups, offshoots, guarding the pulpits, disassociating the church from radical fringe groups, and revival to offset the "different gospel."

C. R. Perry, president of the British Union Conference, addressed some of these issues in an editorial that his constituency entitled *Waco and More Important Matters:* "Waco represented an offshoot, of an offshoot, of an offshoot of the Seventh-day Adventist Church, and what happened there is alien to the teachings and practices of the church. Our teachings are clear on the time and manner of Jesus' second coming. Those who study the Scriptures in the light of what Jesus Christ Himself taught concerning His return to the earth will not be deceived by the claims of antichrists and charlatans such as David Koresh. The wolf comes but to steal and destroy. Those whose faith is anchored in the Lord shall not be shaken by every wind of doctrine."

One of the lessons we must learn, especially those of us who may be prone to be the target of fringe groups that spend their time criticizing the church and its leadership, is how not to be trapped into giving a platform to individuals with extreme views that undermine the authority and teaching of the church.

Having said this, we do not seek to deny any member the right to freedom of speech or freedom to worship according to the dictates of his or her own conscience. On balance, the church has a right also to protect the new believers from those who seek to molest them with their special brand of "righteousness."

It is unchristian for the religiously disaffected to lead others down the slippery slope into ruin.

◆◆◆

At least 18 Britons were inside the compound during the initial raid. Fifteen of them died in the fire. And six of those 15 belonged to the Samuel Henry family.

CHAPTER FOURTEEN

THE BUCKS BEHIND THE BEHAVIOR

"Drop dead!" Those certainly weren't the words the apostle Peter spoke to Ananias and Sapphira, but the net effect was the same.

The early Christian church represented what would today be termed an "intentional community." Admittedly, the punishment that Ananias and Sapphira received does not appear to be because they refused to sell all for the Christian cause. Rather, it was because they pledged a certain amount, then changed their minds, and in effect lied to the Holy Spirit.

But regardless of their punishment, the early church did set a clear precedent for the financial sacrifice expected today from members of some churches and many cults.

"Neither said any of them that ought of the things which he possessed was his own; but they had all things in common. . . . Neither was there any among them that lacked: for as many as were possessors of lands or houses sold them, and brought the prices of the things that were sold, and laid them down at the apostles' feet: and distribution was made unto every man according as he had need" (Acts 4:32-35).

In the case of the Branch Davidians, the stockpiling of nearly $200,000 worth of weapons in less than a year's time left many people, including the government, wondering where David Koresh got his money.

"A financial riddle lurks behind the events at the besieged Branch Davidian compound," wrote one newspaper reporter. "How did an obscure religious sect manage to feed, clothe, house, and heavily arm dozens of devotees, with no obvious sources of income?"

One man who lived with the Davidians for two months said that Koresh did not solicit contributions. The London man paid $40 a month for room and board but said, "I never saw any interaction of money between disciples and Koresh. I don't know where he got his money from. . . . That's the weird thing. You see he can afford all these things, and none of his people seemed like they had a lot of money. There's something fishy here."

◆◆◆

The Branch Davidians owned the sprawling Ranch Apocalypse complex free and clear. The 77-acre spread, valued at $122,000 on the McLennan County tax rolls, was part of 941 acres once owned by the Davidians.

Records show that since 1961 the Davidians never borrowed against the property, nor were any collateral-secured loans to either the Davidians or Koresh registered at the courthouse, where they normally would have been recorded.

However, the fact that the Davidian organization had no debt did not mean its members totally avoided red ink. At least two of his followers maxed out their credit cards for their leader.

Two cult members jointly owned a $350,000 home that Koresh used in California, and they were trying to arrange a $500,000 home equity loan on the house just before the siege. Both had numerous credit cards, with payments ranging as high as $10,000 per month.

A gun-dealing couple, who sold more than $50,000 worth of

weapons to Koresh, described him as an "average Joe" with a penchant for collecting guns, boats, sports cars, and motorcycles. They should have known, since they visited him at the compound as often as four times a week.

"Sometimes he'd call up and say, 'Let's go fishing; I got a new boat,'" one of them said. "Sometimes we'd listen to a little Bible study. That was fine." Like most merchants, they were happy to give a $50,000 customer special treatment.

Other reports claimed that except for the large cache of expensive and illegal weapons, David Koresh and his followers actually lived quite modestly. They collected decades-old cars and recycled building materials, fell behind on property taxes, and purchased food in bulk with cash, food stamps, or other public aid. Furnishings in the compound were comfortable but not plush. Although amenities included a swimming pool, the latest in high-tech sound equipment, a fleet of 30 go-carts, and a TV satellite dish, they had no indoor plumbing.

David Koresh profitted by seizing (or accepting the contributions, depending on your viewpoint!) the assets of his followers. Some cult members tithed on a regular basis, and others sold their possessions to follow "the lamb."

Cult member Steve Schneider told federal investigators over the phone, "We all tithe; we work hard and save money."

"When they joined him, they gave up all their personal goods and money and sold their homes," said Dan Hartnett, associate director of the ATF, the agency that made the initial raid. "And the money went to Koresh."

Certain members could keep some of their possessions, another federal investigator said. However, all cult members had to donate substantially to the Branch Davidian treasury.

Another source of cult income was the salaries of those employed outside the compound. Some cult members, including a Harvard-trained lawyer and a letter carrier, reportedly turned over their paychecks to Koresh on a regular basis. "Good salaries earned on the outside were plowed back into the sect," said Rick

Ross, a cult deprogrammer in Phoenix who has worked with several former Branch Davidians.

Millionaire Paul Fatta, who barely escaped the shoot-out while en route to a gun show, estimated that he gave at least $50,000 to support the cult and David Koresh. Given the descriptions of the way Koresh tossed money around in Hollywood, one would have to wonder if Fatta may have donated considerably more than he wanted to admit.

Some elderly cult members had little or nothing to contribute. Court records showed that one 75-year-old cult member had an annual income of only $509 per year. A 77-year-old woman who had joined the cult 20 years earlier had already given most of her money to the cult coffers and largely depended on the cult's generosity.

Some of the Davidians' support seemed to come through food stamps and other assistance programs. As mentioned earlier, Koresh never allowed his name to be listed as the father of his many illegitimate children, and he had a good financial reason for such behavior.

A former clerk at the Waco Sam's Warehouse was quoted as saying of the Branch Davidians, "They used to come in here and buy all sorts of staples—things like a couple hundred pounds of pinto beans, cases of powdered milk, millet—you know, survival food. They mostly used food stamps. A lot of his 'wives' were registered for welfare."

Food stamp laws provide up to $370 per month for a four-person household. Those who apply for food stamps need not have a permanent address to get them. Even if you do have a permanent address, nobody comes to check it out. Eligibility is based on a variety of criteria, but one thing seems certain. Koresh saw to it that his "wives" were eligible, and food-stamp income provided a significant amount of support for the compound.

In addition to food stamps, it seems quite likely that Koresh's "wives" also collected cash welfare. That may never be known for sure because the agencies involved keep such information confidential.

◆◆◆

When Koresh first joined the Branch Davidians, he was penniless to say the least. It wasn't until he wrested final control from arch-rival George Roden that he finally obtained the funding to upgrade Mount Carmel and bankroll his lifestyle, numerous recruiting trips, and massive weapons buildup.

Did the Davidians ever control how Koresh spent their money? It doesn't seem likely. After all, he inherited the legacy of Houteff and the Rodens, which was one of absolute control. He was the prophet, he was "God," and no one need question what he did.

A portion of the Branch Davidians' constitution under Ben Roden, which no doubt shifted to Koresh upon his rise to power, gives some indication of the absolute power always vested in the Branch Davidians' leader: "Therefore as members of the Branch Davidian Seventh-day Adventist association, the membership appoints (Hosea 1:11) the president Ben L. Roden, as holding in his sole possession all legal, moral, and scriptural ownership and rights of the association, all its assets and holdings, and to operate the same for the furtherance of the association's work at home and abroad: to execute and administrate the entire balances of the association, to judge and make final judgment in all matters concerning the association's works, assets, and holdings, and to be its chief and sole administrator."

Later, Koresh put his own interpretation on Roden's statements. "It means that the prophet owns everything—your house, your money, even your underwear."

◆◆◆

Forcing followers into economic dependence is just one more means of gaining and retaining total control over their lives, according to Eric Hoffer. "Economic dependence is maintained by centralizing economic power and by a deliberately created scarcity of the necessities of life," he wrote. "Social self-sufficiency is discouraged by crowded housing or communal quarters, and by enforced daily participation in public functions. Ruthless censorship of literature, art, music and science prevents even the creative few from living self-sufficient lives" *(The True Believer,* p. 118).

The Branch Davidians chose to give David Koresh everything—their minds, their houses, their money, and in the case of the women, even their underwear.

Through their tithes, the sale of their homes, their paychecks, credit cards, food stamps and/or welfare money, they made it possible for him to do what he did and become what he became. Without them, he could never have done it. And so, ultimately, they provided the bucks behind the behavior.

CHAPTER FIFTEEN

SINNER WITHOUT EQUAL

"If the Bible is true, then I'm Christ," David Koresh asserted. But he also told a reporter at the Waco *Tribune-Herald* that he was a "sinner without equal."

If you wonder how a person can claim to be Christ and a sinner without equal at the same time, you're not alone.

"He was a gun-toting, spellbinding, self-anointed biblical wizard with a passion for rock music and women," wrote one newspaper reporter. "A sinful Messiah, he called himself, pointing to a bizarre lifestyle that included an alleged obsession for young girls and an apocalyptic death wish. A prophet with a pistol. A lamb with an attitude."

If Koresh were Christ, it was with a dramatic difference. He was the sinful messiah, he told his followers. "The first Jesus was pure and sinless. How could He judge anyone?" Koresh asked. Claiming to be the new Jesus Christ, Koresh cursed like a sailor and admitted lusting after women. And not from afar.

Ruling Ranch Apocalypse like he was a god, he told his followers, "God allows men to be born into sin. It is natural for man to sin. If you're going to be fair, you've got to give man a way out."

Nearly all former cult members no longer believe that Koresh was Christ, but they all agree on one thing: he was sinful.

Claiming to be the sinful messiah may be a new twist. But

when David Koresh called himself the "Messiah," he was treading where others had definitely been before. A number of cult leaders, criminals, and other psychotics have claimed, throughout the years, to have some form of divinity. Jim Jones of the People's Temple in Guyana and Yahweh ben Yahweh of the Nation of Yahweh in Miami are just two such impostors. One cult researcher states that currently as many as 1,200 persons refer to themselves as the "Messiah."

"What surprises me most about David Koresh's claim to be the Messiah," remarked one minister from the pulpit during the siege, "is not so much that he claims to be the Messiah, but the number of people who have called in to TV and radio talk shows during the standoff to say 'He's not the Messiah; I am!' "

"You could go outside the New York Public Library, and there would be 20 Christs, a couple of Pauls, and some Peters," commented Dr. Jonas Rappeport, an expert in forensic psychiatry. "These are terribly sick people, so no one follows them, no one pays attention to them. But then there are these chaps who are less ill, and who are charismatic and can get people to follow them, like this one in Texas and Jim Jones."

◆◆◆

Since early Christianity, countless false messiahs have seen the opportunity and have run with it. All were self-proclaimed emissaries of God. All had a bad attitude toward the status quo. All were convinced of their inherent right to rule over others. And all adopted a methodology that became nearly standardized: isolate believers, mesmerize them with apocalyptic bombast, and enforce unquestioning obedience to them as leader.

Christ predicted that many false messiahs would appear, "claiming to work miracles, and declaring that the time of the deliverance of the Jewish nation has come," wrote Ellen White. "These will mislead many. Christ's words were fulfilled. Between His death and the siege of Jerusalem many false messiahs appeared. But this warning was given also to those who live in this age of the world. The same deceptions practiced prior to the destruction of Jerusalem have been practiced through the ages, and will be practiced again" *(The Desire of Ages,* p. 628).

◆◆◆

"America has been fertile soil for messiahs," wrote one newspaper reporter. "We grow them like corn. Throughout our history, throngs of ordinary-seeming people have dropped office ledgers and plows to follow the Joseph Smiths and the Jim Joneses into the wilderness to await the Day of Reckoning."

Dr. Rappeport offered one possible explanation for the crowded field of would-be messiahs. "If you're going to have a delusion, you're not going to imagine you're Joe Jerk," he commented.

Defendants in criminal trials have been known to claim to be the Godhead, as in the case of George Roden. Some are truly deluded, while others are looking for a way out by reason of insanity.

In addition to his "bold gold" business cards proclaiming himself to be the "Messiah," Koresh frequently signed correspondence "Yahweh Koresh." (Yahweh is the holiest Jewish term for God.)

According to J. Gordon Melton, editor of the *Encyclopedia of American Religions,* few religious leaders claim to be God Himself. More likely or plausible claims are to be a prophet or to have some special pipeline to God.

Nonetheless, numerous other small sects out there hold beliefs that are mirror images of Koresh and Jim Jones, according to Larry Nichols, coauthor of the *Dictionary of Cults, Sects, Religions, and the Occult.* "All of them are getting personal messages from God about the imminent end of time," he says.

But being the "Messiah" is heady stuff. For, as the saying goes, "power currupts, and absolute power corrupts absolutely." For some cult leaders, and David Koresh seemed to be no exception, proclaiming themselves to be "God" goes to their head.

Koresh's followers were no doubt strengthened in their faith by the injuries that their leader sustained in the initial shoot-out. Gunshot wounds in the hand and side, to their minds, would have paralleled Jesus' wounds.

"He is wounded like Jesus. That carries theological weight," commented a psychiatrist briefing federal agents. "That would indicate to his followers that he is a Messianic figure."

Koresh had also burned a cross into his chest, according to reports of several former followers.

According to cult expert Ronald Enroth, Koresh's flock faithfully followed him until the end. When the FBI hit, "he probably told them, 'Here it is, friends; this is the beginning of what I told you would *happen,'*" Enroth remarked. "And that only made his claim of Messiahship more real to them."

Koresh appeared to be trying to fulfill prophecy by celebrating a Passover during the siege. Calling it a "high holy day," Koresh ominously told his group that it would be the last Passover that they would celebrate together.

His religious pronouncements to his followers came between negotiation sessions with the FBI, in which Koresh seesawed between shouting profanities and speaking of a peaceful end to the crisis.

Initially Koresh had shied away from publicly acknowledging that he considered himself to be Christ. "I'd be lying if I said yes," he told the Waco *Tribune-Herald.* "I'd be lying if I said no."

But in a later interview, he confirmed his claim. "If the Bible is true, I'm Christ," he said. "But so what? What's so great about being Christ? A man nailed to the cross. A man acquainted with grief."

According to a document released by Marc Breault, "from 1983 to 1985 Howell saw himself merely as a prophet, someone whom he termed 'the seventh angel's messenger.' In 1985 Howell saw himself as Cyrus, the latter-day king who would lead God's people until God esablished His kingdom on earth. In 1988 Howell became the Lamb of God portrayed in Revelation 5. At this stage Howell believed that the lamb of Revelation was different than Jesus Christ, the Lamb of God. To Vernon's thinking, the lamb of Revelation was Cyrus, or the king. During this stage Howell became the Son of God, but maintained a separate identity than that of Jesus Christ. Finally, in 1989, Howell merged the lamb of Revelation with Jesus Christ. To him, they became one and the same person."

It seems that Koresh was not quite sure who he thought he was at the end, and during the decade from 1983 to 1993 he changed who he was claiming to be five or more times!

Whatever he was, the Reverend John McDonough of Akron, Ohio, had some advice for his followers: "If faith comes through hearing, then I better make sure I have examined the credentials of the one who is speaking."

◆◆◆

Koresh's followers seemed to have accorded him prophetic status—and then divinity. Whatever conclusions they reached seem to have occurred in a less than rational manner. The objective observer has to recognize some major discrepancies between David Koresh and Jesus Christ.

If Koresh were the reincarnation of Jesus, as he claimed to be, a tremendous and extremely negative transformation in personality occurred between the ascension and the surprise reincarnation. Listed below are some of the reasons David Koresh could not possibly have been the Messiah:

1. The attitude of Koresh toward his "persecutors." At the cross Jesus prayed, "Father, forgive them; for they know not what they do" (Luke 23:34). Even as He lay in pain and death was only hours away, He still cared about the salvation of the Roman soldiers pounding spikes into His hands.

In contrast, David Koresh invoked repeated threats of judgment and harsh retribution on the FBI for their dealings with him.

"Please do not harm my Lamb," one message from the compound had warned the FBI. Subsequent messages threatened that the FBI would be "devoured by fire" if they hurt Koresh. The FBI described the entire unpublished letter as one of vengeful reprisal against those who defy "the lamb."

"Who will atone for your rejecting my spirit? I am your God, and you will bow under my feet," he wrote to the FBI. "Do you know my seals? Do you dare call me a liar? . . . I am your life and your death."

2. Sin is foreign to God. According to the Bible, Christ lived a sinless life here on earth so that we might live a righteous life in Him.

"For he hath made him to be sin for us, who knew no sin; that we might be made the righteousness of God in him" (2 Cor. 5:21).

"And ye know that he was manifested to take away our sins; and in him is no sin" (1 John 3:5).

If sin was so repulsive to God that the only appropriate penalty for it was death, and if God could not change that penalty even though it meant the sacrifice and death of His Son, wouldn't it seem a little strange that God suddenly changed His mind?

If there was war in heaven, and if God had had to throw Lucifer out because of his self-centered ambitions, does it seem likely that God would reincarnate His Son in the person of David Koresh to desecrate every one of the Ten Commandments?

3. Christ's sacrifice was sufficient. If you accept the claims of Koresh, Christ's sacrifice becomes meaningless! Koresh claimed that God must have made a mistake, because people couldn't relate to the sinless Christ. So Koresh was the answer to the dilemma.

But the Bible says clearly that Christ's sacrifice was sufficient.

"And all things are of God, who hath reconciled us to himself by Jesus Christ, and hath given to us the ministry of reconciliation" (2 Cor. 5:18).

"For God so loved the world, that he gave his only begotten Son, that whosoever believeth in him should not perish, but have everlasting life" (John 3:16).

4. Christ is a merciful and faithful high priest. Koresh claimed that Christ could not judge or even understand humanity, since He had not known sin. However, this directly contradicts the Bible.

"Wherefore in all things it behoved him to be made like unto his brethren, that he might be a merciful and faithful high priest in things pertaining to God, to make reconciliation for the sins of the people. For in that he himself hath suffered being tempted, he is able to succour them that are tempted" (Heb. 2:17, 18).

Was Koresh Jesus reincarnated? Did God change His mind and decide that sin was OK after all?

Not according to 1 John 3:8: "He that committeth sin is of the devil; for the devil sinneth from the beginning. For this purpose the Son of God was manifested, that he might destroy the works of the devil."

Some think that Koresh was devil-possessed. For those who have studied the character of God as revealed in the Bible, the chances of Koresh's hearing a voice from God saying, "I will give thee Madonna" seem phenomenally less than zero.

One reporter, requesting a change from the dentist's drill, squealing rabbits, and other grating noises used in psychological warfare against the cult, suggested a verse from Elvis Presley's 1963 number 3 hit, "Devil in Disguise," in which he sang about a woman who behaved like an angel but was in reality a devil in disguise.

One thing is for sure. The teachings of David Koresh directly contradicted the Bible. They were not from God.

◆◆◆

George Roden's, Koresh's onetime arch-rival for leadership of the cult, may have had the last word on the subject. When George heard of the standoff, he called a press conference at the psychiatric hospital where he now resides.

"I believe he is deluded," George, the "legally insane" man began, though he never sounded saner. "I believe he is deluded about himself. He is not Jesus Christ . . . any more than Satan is."

CHAPTER SIXTEEN

THE ENFORCERS

David Koresh called them his "Mighty Men." The paranoid cult leader had handpicked them to enforce his bizarre rules and to protect himself from any intruders or enemies.

Known also as his Royal Guard, they all received training to use AK-47s and M-16s. They were the men of the compound—men who existed solely for the purpose of obeying his commands.

If the truth were known, Koresh desperately needed his commandos in order to survive. Typically he surrounded himself with men of expertise, means, and intelligence. They were highly educated and skilled in various fields such as computers, law, music, and building trades.

"The uncanny powers of a leader manifest themselves not so much in the hold he has on the masses as in his ability to dominate and almost bewitch a small group of able men," wrote Eric Hoffer. "These men must be fearless, proud, intelligent, and capable of organizing and running large-scale undertakings, and yet they must submit wholly to the will of the leader, draw their inspiration and driving force from him, and glory in this submission" *(The True Believer,* p. 106).

Although Koresh was gifted in manipulation and mind control, his obsession for control—manifested in his buildup of weapons and ammunition—was not something that he could accomplish alone. Therefore he handpicked his personal assistants—his most trusted being Steve Schneider, 43, a silver-tongued and articulate religion teacher; and Douglas Wayne Martin, a Harvard-educated lawyer. Both men died with Koresh in the Waco fire that reduced the compound to rubble.

◆◆◆

So, what was life like for this inner circle of enforcers?

The rigidly structured days began early. The ringing of a bell roused the men around 5:15 a.m. They underwent military training by doing exercises, running a two-mile obstacle course, and then gathering for a plain breakfast of cooked cereal set out by the women. Koresh, meanwhile, always slept in late, usually showing up around 3:00 p.m.

Those, such as David Jones, 38 (a mail carrier in town), who held down regular jobs in the community left for work while the others endured hours of Bible study, pulled guard duty at a flea-infested shack on the edge of the property, assisted with construction duties, and dug tunnels around the compound.

All mass movements use action as a means of unification, and the Branch Davidians were no exception. Whether the faithful are clearing land, building cities, or renovating a Ranch Apocalypse, they are kept busy, incessantly busy.

This "call for action evokes an eager response in the frustrated," wrote Eric Hoffer. "For the frustrated see in action a cure for all that ails them. It brings self-forgetting and it gives them a sense of purpose and worth" *(ibid.,* p. 112).

For the Branch Davidians, it may have helped them forget their unpleasant surroundings. One of the lucky ones, millionaire Paul Fatta often attended gun shows, and he traveled extensively to purchase weapons and ammunition. He was reportedly attending a gun show in Austin on February 28, the day federal agents raided the compound, and he did not return during the siege. However, he did later surrender to Texas Rangers in Houston after the holocaust.

◆◆◆

Many of the Mighty Men of Koresh's cult were likable, sincere, and were often described as devout. But the strange thread tying them all together seemed to be that they all were committed to a common vision. They all seemed to be looking for a grand event, a confrontation.

And true to militaristic fashion, if someone refused to follow orders, he was punished. Marc Breault, one of Koresh's former Mighty Men, said that "anytime anyone disobeyed, he'd [Koresh] have the whole camp fast. Everyone was always hungry.

"Koresh said someday we'd be in a war—and we had to get used to food deprivation because there would be a time when everyone would be hungry, and we would survive longer because we would be used to it."

One of the main functions of Koresh's Mighty Men was to know how to use a weapon. Those who were experts taught the others, including women of all ages, how to shoot.

Because of his fear of a confrontation with the authorities, Koresh's goal at the compound was to make everyone a crack shot. Marc Breault said, "He knew he was on a collision course with the government, and he conditioned us to think the same thing—and it was one fight we were determined not to lose."

◆◆◆

All Koresh's Mighty Men gave up their personal property or whatever assets they had to the cult leader. In fact, members willingly surrendered most of their rights while Koresh built his own kingdom on 77 acres.

Throughout the siege many wondered, "How could bright,

able people end up as top lieutenants to David Koresh?"

For some, being a cult member must have become an impossible situation to get out of. They felt that they had no one to turn to or nowhere to turn. And perhaps they also denied the fact that anything as fatal as the final fire could actually happen.

For example, Doug Martin, who represented the Davidians in negotiations with federal officers, saw three of his children leave the compound as well as his wife, Sheila. One wonders what he was thinking—perhaps that he, too, would leave at a more opportune time?

For years before the standoff, Martin maintained a law practice near the Mount Carmel compound. As a 1977 Harvard Law School graduate, people often described him as nice and personable, although somewhat inexperienced. Those who knew the family said that they were quite religious, and definitely not mainstream conformists.

Nevertheless, those living at Mount Carmel were expected to abide by the strict rules enforced by Koresh.

While Koresh was allowed to drink alcohol, his followers were not. Vegetarians, they also avoided caffeine and dressed plainly in clothes they made themselves. The women wore no makeup. And the men, women, and children prayed and studied the Bible, sometimes in sessions that lasted 15 hours straight.

Claiming to have biblical license to take any man's wife, Koresh began sleeping with the wives of his top lieutenants. The men were devastated, but they allowed this degrading practice because they viewed Koresh as their "sinful messiah."

The Mighty Men in the compound wore black clothing sewn by the wives they had given to Koresh. Interestingly enough, soon after Koresh took the wives from his Mighty Men, he began to allow the men to drink beer, which seemed to anesthetize them to their pain and suffering at not being allowed any intimacy with their own wives.

Neighbors living nearby commented that those inside must have it "pretty good" because of all the dune buggies, motorcycles, and four-wheelers that they had stashed inside the barbed-wire fences. But the neighbors did notice that the atmosphere within the compound seemed anything but relaxed. An armed guard stood at the gate, and Koresh reportedly had someone guarding his quarters 24 hours a day.

◆◆◆

What were the guards protecting?

Federal officials believe that as Koresh's top lieutenants, the Mighty Men may have helped their leader a final time by killing some of the Branch Davidians who tried to escape the final fire.

The autopsies of several bodies revealed bullet wounds, and one of them was singed in such a way that led authorities to speculate that he might have been trying to flee the burning compound.

The Mighty Men believed that they were like the mighty men in the Old Testament, the select warriors surrounding King David. According to the Bible, "these also are the chief of the mighty men whom David had, who strengthened themselves with him in his kingdom, and with all Israel, to make him king, according to the word of the Lord concerning Israel" (1 Chron. 11:10).

The difference in Koresh's band of men and King David's of old was the leader to whom they pledged their allegiance. King David followed and obeyed God (much of the time), but David Koresh eventually made himself "God" and disregarded the plain teachings of Scripture.

Former cult members say that although some of Koresh's Mighty Men professed great respect for him, they in fact hated him for taking their wives, and also for his alleged cruelty to their children. During their final months, the men lived in what has been described as an anguished celibacy. Finally, during the standoff, up to 30 persons inside the compound had expressed a desire to leave if they could be sure of their legal standing.

However, after they made their wish known, precious few were actually allowed to leave.

In the end, six of the 20 Mighty Men did escape the blaze, perhaps finding themselves not so willing to die for their leader after all.

Fortunately, the final reckoning of these men will be left to a fair and all-knowing God, who feels the innermost longings of the soul, sees and understands impossible circumstances, and hears the faintest acknowledgment of Him through the confessions of a repentant heart.

Chapter Seventeen

How Unlucky Can You Get?

Sixteen-year-old Misty Ferguson may have survived the fatal fire at the Waco compound, but she's still a victim. FBI agents dragged her from the blazing compound, and, having been overcome by burns and shock, she was rushed to Parkland Hospital in Dallas.

"I don't know if she has any family or if they all perished in the flames. No one has been to visit her. It's as though she lost everything at Waco," said a nurse at the hospital.

Some say Misty is lucky to be alive. Especially the case-hardened sheriff's deputies and Texas Rangers who, struck dumb with horror, had to perform the gruesome task of recovering bodies from the Waco disaster—including those of small children huddled in the debris.

Others aren't so sure.

With the sect consumed by fire, the tales of life in Mount Carmel come mostly from the mouths of children. And as stories from survivors, former Davidians, and a psychiatric report on the children have confirmed, the Ranch Apocalypse experience was one of deprivation and fear. Denied traditional family bonds and exposed to Koresh's teachings, the children who left the compound before the gruesome end may face lifelong psychological and spiritual problems.

One can only imagine the confusion and fear that the kids experienced, especially during the last few weeks on the compound. Those who later died endured extreme psychological pressure, such as the loud noises inflicted by the FBI. And like disc jockeys from hell, the FBI also blared progressively more irritating tunes and sounds at the nearly 100 well-armed Branch Davidian members.

In this war of nerves, 22 children ate, slept, and presumably played. Their immature minds probably wondered what in the world was going on. Perhaps it occasionally seemed like a 24-hour carnival. And to add to the turmoil—near the end of the siege—bright lights shone through the windows, which, no doubt, made it difficult for the keyed-up children to sleep.

◆◆◆

A 12-year-old Michigan girl, Kiri Jewell, whose mother perished in the flames, was one of the lucky ones. Her father, disc jockey David Jewell of Niles, sought the court's help in gaining custody of his daughter who had lived with her mother in the cult's headquarters for four years. He had his daughter removed from the compound in 1992, when he discovered that she was being groomed to be one of David Koresh's wives and that her mother didn't object.

In a television interview on the *Phil Donahue Show,* Kiri said, "We were taught to put a gun in our mouths and how to kill ourselves by taking cyanide. In the compound were lots and lots of guns and enough food to feed all of us for months."

She also confided in her father how Koresh had paddled her because she didn't learn a Bible verse or chapter fast enough. David Jewell also said that she told him of other instances of abuse that "they just aren't ready to talk about yet."

◆◆◆

Former cult members have told many tales of child abuse in

the compound. For "sins" as small as spilling milk the children were struck with a wooden paddle known as the "helper." It was "full-contact" whipping, too, enough to leave its marks on a baby's buttocks. Often cult members used a large spoon with a straight handle and almost spatulalike bowl.

Former cult member Michelle Tom told a Michigan court that Howell hit Tarah Tom, her daughter, on her buttocks with the wooden spoon for more than 30 minutes in 1988. The baby's "sin"? Crying when put on Koresh's lap, the affidavit said.

"My baby was 8 months old at the time, and when he finished, her bottom was badly bruised and bleeding," Tom wrote.

A former cult member who does not wish to be identified saw Tarah after the whipping and said, "Her bottom was completely black and blue."

◆◆◆

David Koresh didn't just punish the children of other Branch Davidians. He was particularly harsh to his son, Cyrus, a bright-eyed child of 7 at the time he died in the Waco inferno.

During a 1986 Bible study in Palestine, Texas, Cyrus, then about 1 year old, began crying. Having been left alone in a bus, he was wet, cold, and hungry. Irritated at the disruption, Koresh made several trips to the bus to spank his son. Each attack reportedly lasted several minutes. The boy's screams from the bus haunted the church, a former cult member said.

When Cyrus was about 3, Koresh decided that he was not happy with the way his legal wife Rachel was raising their child. So he took Cyrus out to California and put him under the care of Nicole Gent from Australia. When Cyrus refused to call his new caretaker "mommy," Howell made Cyrus sleep in the garage where, he told the unfortunate child, large rats prowled and ate naughty kids!

And yet, mysteriously, many of the 21 children released before the horrible fire seemed to be relatively well-adjusted and adequately educated. And a videotape given to authorities showed the children who remained inside the compound to be outwardly in good condition.

◆◆◆

Psychologists who treat people raised in cults say that younger children may actually flourish in the groups, which function like an extended family. But when they come into their own at around 10 and begin to rebel, they often receive severe punishment.

For the children in the Mount Carmel compound, the harsh discipline started early. Their messiah taught the parents that they should spank their 8-month-old children.

Most mothers would intervene if someone severely beat their child, but the Branch Davidian women seemed to retreat.

In the Waco compound many of the children had no recorded father. Although Koresh reputedly fathered some 10 children, he didn't want anyone recording the babies born to unwed Branch Davidian women lest it attract unwanted attention from the authorities.

◆◆◆

Other signs of abuse appeared. For example, one former cult member remembered that the young boys could not sleep late in the mornings but were roused out of bed at 5:30 and sent down to the "gym." Although the little girls could sleep as late as they wanted, they often went hungry.

"Sometimes dinner for the 100 or so cult members only amounted to popcorn—and the lucky might get a tad of oil or a dash of salt—or rarely—a piece of fruit," Marc Breault recalled.

And then there were the wrenchingly long hours of "Bible study," which often amounted to Koresh's ramblings regarding the book of Revelation. He also considered himself an authority on marriage and sex—and lectured with graphic detail.

Girls as young as 11 received a plastic Star of David, signifying that they had the "light" and were ready to have sex with the cult leader at his whim.

◆◆◆

A team of therapists said that these were some of the things that the children who left the compound and survived the inferno told them about their lives inside Ranch Apocalypse. Those interviewed ranged from ages 4 through 11.

Studies done on children in cults has found that the treatment of children varies widely among groups and depends largely on the mental state of the leader.

Certainly one of the lessons learned from the Waco incident regarding children is that mothers and fathers mold society and the future. "The nobler the aims, the higher the mental and spiritual endowments, and the better developed the physical powers of the parents, the better will be the life equipment they give their children. In cultivating that which is best in themselves, parents are exerting an influence to mold society and to uplift future generations" (*Mind, Character, and Personality,* vol. 1, p. 139).

◆◆◆

The children of David Koresh's doomsday cult were apparently mentally prepared for the final battle. Surviving members have told authorities that when bullets rained down on the commune the children remained calm, believing the shoot-out was a prophecy fulfilled.

And yet when the end came, they all died in an inferno that engulfed their surroundings and even destroyed much of the evidence that would lead experts to know exactly how they had perished.

Chapter Eighteen

Why Adventists Were Vulnerable

Have you ever felt that life is spinning out of control? Has the world ever looked strange and scary? Has it ever seemed that none of the old values applies anymore?

Join the club—or the cult!

When people get overwhelmed and frustrated by the uncertainties of life, they may gravitate to an individual or organization that promises a secret key to security and happiness. So says a group of professional cult watchers.

David Koresh was a master of persuasion. But if you believe Eric Hoffer: "Propaganda by itself succeeds mainly with the frustrated. Their throbbing fears, hopes and passions crowd at the portals of their senses and get between them and the outside world. They cannot see but what they have already imagined, and it is the music of their own souls they hear in the impassioned words of the propagandist" *(The True Believer,* p. 98).

"Propaganda by itself, however skillful, cannot keep people persuaded once they have ceased to believe," he continued. "To maintain itself, a mass movement has to order things so that when the people no longer believe, they can be made to believe by force. . . .

"It is probably as true that violence breeds fanaticism as that fanaticism begets violence. It is often impossible to tell which came first. Both those who employ violence and those subject to it are likely to develop a fanatical state of mind" *(ibid.,* pp. 98, 99).

◆◆◆

The question on the lips of many—Adventist and non-Adventist alike—is the same: Why would anybody follow David Koresh?

His double standards and bizarre doctrines about the "sinful Messiah," fornication and adultery, self-inflicted hardship, and "raising children to rule the world" hardly sound appealing at first—or even second—glance.

Then why did nearly 100 followers hole up with him, vowing to stick it out to the end? And why did committed followers on the outside proclaim, "I wish I could have died with them. That's where the truth was"?

In short, why were so many of the Branch Davidians former Seventh-day Adventists? And why were Seventh-day Adventists vulnerable to the likes of David Koresh?

To answer the first question, Koresh and the Davidians recruited almost exclusively from the ranks of Seventh-day Adventists. From the 1930s on, the Davidians believed that they had a special message to the Seventh-day Adventist Church. They distributed material aggressively at camp meetings and at any other Adventist gatherings where they could find people to take their pamphlets.

Because the Davidians recruited almost exclusively from Adventist ranks, it stands to reason that their organization would consist primarily of ex-Seventh-day Adventists.

Despite nearly 60 years of recruiting from Seventh-day Adventist membership, the number of actual defectors was statistically insignificant. For example, some estimates place the current number of Davidians worldwide to be about 2,000. If those 2,000 Davidians came from a grand total of 7 million Adventists worldwide, the Davidians successfully recruited approximately .03

percent of the total Adventist Church membership. Of course, each individual is significant in God's eyes, but the point here is that the Davidians did not experience overwhelming or even a threatening level of success in adding Seventh-day Adventists to their numbers.

◆◆◆

Below we list some factors that may have made Seventh-day Adventists more susceptible to the Branch Davidian doctrine.

1. Openness to the idea of a modern-day prophet. Adventists, having accepted the idea of a modern-day prophet in the person of Ellen G. White, might be more ready to accept the appearance of another modern-day prophet than would members of some other denominations. If you went up to a Baptist or a Methodist and told him or her that you were a prophet, he or she might believe that the gift of prophecy ended with the apostles and tell you to forget it. But Seventh-day Adventists believe that the gift of prophecy will extend until the end of time.

They find one biblical support for this belief in Joel 2:28: "And it shall come to pass afterward, that I will pour out my spirit upon all flesh; and your sons and your daughters shall prophesy, your old men shall dream dreams, your young men shall see visions."

Since immediately after this verse Joel speaks of signs in the heavens that seem to parallel those that Jesus also predicted would happen at the end of the world, Adventists conclude that it is reasonable to assume that the gift of prophecy will remain until the end of time.

Even stronger than that argument is the Adventist belief that the gift of prophecy will represent one of the identifying marks of God's final church.

For a description of these identifying marks, Adventists turn to Revelation: "And the dragon was wroth with the woman, and went to make war with the remnant of her seed, which keep the commandments of God, and have the testimony of Jesus Christ" (12:17).

And for a definition of the testimony of Jesus, we Adventists turn to a parallel passage: "For the testimony of Jesus is the spirit of prophecy" (Rev. 19:10).

Much Adventist theology rests on these few texts, for we use them to support the belief that the Adventist Church is God's remnant church, since it meets the criteria described in Revelation.

Adventists keep the commandments of God, with a literal interpretation of the Ten Commandments, and especially the seventh-day Sabbath.

And Adventists believe that God gave the gift of prophecy to the Seventh-day Adventist Church in the writings of Ellen G. White. And since the gift of prophecy will continue to the end of time, as God sees fit, that does leave the door open for other potential prophets.

David Koresh saw that door, and walked right through it. Branch Davidians have always claimed to have a prophet among them—from Victor Houteff to Ben and Lois Roden to George Roden. But the gift of prophecy is meaningless unless a community recognizes and accepts that individual, holding the prophet in high esteem and hearing his or her authoritative voice.

The Seventh-day Adventist Church rejected the Branch Davidian prophets, instead turning to Isaiah 8:20 for the definition of a true prophet: "To the law and to the testimony: if they speak not according to this word, it is because there is no light in them."

But many young Seventh-day Adventists were unaware of the history of the Branch Davidians, and Koresh loved to pose as a Seventh-day Adventist. An avid student of Ellen White's writings himself, he found that his photographic memory served him well in quoting her as well as most of the Scripture that he had memorized.

Koresh was disfellowshipped from the Tyler Seventh-day Adventist Church in Texas in 1981, and numerous reports relate his general disdain for the denomination that spurned his supposed prophetic gift. However, even though he was not even a member when he made his recruiting drive in Hawaii, he often made statements to new Adventist converts, such as "we as

Adventists," and drew extensively from the writings of Ellen White to make his points.

Like some others before him (who also ultimately came to naught), Koresh at first claimed that he was a prophet to follow Ellen G. White. However, in more recent years he changed that view and rejected all her writings.

When recruiting, however, Koresh loved to approach conservative young Seventh-day Adventists who were serious about their religion and about the writings of Ellen White. With his extensive knowledge of both Scripture and her writings, one can see how some Adventists who were avid readers of both the Bible and Mrs. White and who knew as yet nothing of his bizarre lifestyle and actual beliefs would have found that seductive.

Those who would tag Seventh-day Adventists themselves as a cult should consider the difference between cult leaders and Ellen White. David Koresh, Jim Jones, and others who have claimed to have prophetic powers propounded new doctrine(s), changing what others had already deduced as orthodox from the Bible. Seventh-day Adventism, on the other hand, rejects the use of writings of Ellen White as a source of new tenets of belief. "The testimonies have not been given to establish new doctrine. The doctrine is established by the Word of God, and the Spirit of Prophecy comes in to bring out the light, revealing new beauties in it, and bringing out here and there details which help in the understanding of the Word of God" (*Ellen G. White: The Australian Years,* p. 68).

Ellen White also expressed her openness to having any doctrines held up to the light of the Scriptures for continued examination. "Truth is eternal," she wrote, "and conflict with error will only make manifest its strength. We should never refuse to examine the Scriptures with those who, we have reason to believe, desire to know what is truth as much as we do. Suppose a brother held a view that differed from yours, and he should come to you, proposing that you sit down with him and make an investigation of that point in the Scriptures; should you rise up, filled with prejudice, and condemn his ideas, while refusing to give him a candid hearing?

"The only right way would be to sit down as Christians and investigate the position presented, in the light of God's word, which will reveal truth and unmask error. To ridicule his ideas would not weaken his position in the least if it were false, or strengthen your position if it were true. If the pillars of our faith will not stand the test of investigation, it is time that we knew it" *(Counsels to Writers and Editors,* p. 44).

2. Openness to the idea of new light. Adventists believe that Adventist pioneers added to the spiritual illumination shining from the Protestant Reformation. Ellen White's book *The Great Controversy,* which describes the struggle between good and evil and between God and Satan, begins by describing an era of spiritual darkness when the masses did not have the Bible available to them.

Following the Dark Ages the Protestant Reformers recovered many teachings now cherished by Protestant churches everywhere, such as a renewed emphasis on salvation by grace. In an effort to open the eyes of church members to the need for continued reform, Ellen White wrote the following, describing the attitude toward "new light" long cherished by the Adventist Church:

"The Reformation did not, as many suppose, end with Luther. It is to be continued to the close of this world's history. Luther had a great work to do in reflecting upon others the light which God permitted to shine upon him; yet he did not receive all the light which was to be given to the world. From that time to this, new light has been continually shining upon the Scriptures, and new truths have been constantly unfolding" *(The Great Controversy,* pp. 148, 149).

The Great Controversy and other Adventist publications all consider the seventh day as Sabbath, the meaning of the earthly sanctuary in describing salvation and pointing to the heavenly sanctuary, and the message of temperance in eating, drinking, and dress as new light, added to the firm foundation laid by such great reformers as Huss, Zwingli, John and Charles Wesley, and Martin Luther.

David Koresh took the idea of new light and ran with it. He may very well have quoted the text "The people that walked in darkness have seen a great light: they that dwell in the land of the shadow of death, upon them hath the light shined" (Isaiah 9:2).

His new light, however, could not have been shining from the Word of God because it directly contradicted Scripture. From an Adventist point of view, there is nothing wrong with the idea of new light. God may choose to reveal even more to His people until the end of time. However, any new understandings must be held up and closely scrutinized by what we already know from the Bible.

"When anyone comes to you with a new doctrine," wrote Ellen White, "you should challenge him to prove it by the word of God. The test is written: 'To the law and to the testimony; if they speak not according to this word, it is because there is no light in them'" *(Signs of the Times,* Nov. 27, 1887).

3. The apocalyptic emphasis. Adventism was born with an end-time perspective. The preaching of William Miller and other heralds of the soon coming of Christ in the early 1800s stirred all America. When the appointed time for Christ's return came and went in the autumn of 1844, nothing could describe the disappointment of the thousands of believers who had waited eagerly for that day.

The faithful few who remained after that great disappointment formed the nucleus of the future Seventh-day Adventist Church. They rediscovered the message given by Christ in Matthew 24:36, 44: "But of that day and hour knoweth no man, no, not the angels of heaven, but my Father only." "Therefore be ye also ready: for in such an hour as ye think not the Son of man cometh."

Although that bitter experience did not immediately cure any Adventist time-setting tendencies until after Ellen White again and again spoke out against predicting the time of Christ's return, the apocalyptic emphasis remained ever present. Vivid caricatures of the beasts of Daniel and Revelation were often used in flyers to attract potential converts to evangelistic meetings, and a fervent message echoed throughout Adventist churches across the nation and eventually the world: "Get ready! Jesus is coming soon!"

The Davidians claimed that they did not deny or dispute Adventist teaching about the soon return of Jesus, only that they had additional knowledge about it. Adventist young people were certainly in tune with the theme of Christ's soon coming, and this may have made them more susceptible to the apocalyptic doctrine of David Koresh.

4. Belief in a coming persecution. David Koresh had a persecution complex. There's no doubt about it. The idea of persecution is perfectly biblical, and you don't have to look in the book of Revelation to find it, either. "Then shall they deliver you up to be afflicted, and shall kill you: and ye shall be hated of all nations for my name's sake. And then shall many be offended, and shall betray one another, and shall hate one another" (Matt. 24:9, 10).

Jesus was talking about the time of the end. The book of Revelation depicts the persecution of the saints in an even more graphic way, and chapters in *The Great Controversy* also describe the persecution that awaits God's people before the final deliverance.

The point here is that although David Koresh's theology may have been bizarre, some of the major themes, such as the idea of a chosen people, confrontation with government over obeying God's laws rather than man's, potential martyrdom, and the whole idea of persecution, are certainly not new to Adventism.

Once Koresh's followers accorded him prophetic or even messianic status, however, he kept adding new and often bizarre interpretations that most of his followers obediently accepted as gospel truth.

5. Belief in the narrow gate. One emphasis some have adduced from Scripture is that the vast majority of people will not be saved. "But as the days of [Noah] were, so shall also the coming of the Son of man be," Christ told His disciples (Matt. 24:37). In the days of Noah only eight persons entered the ark and were saved.

"Enter ye in at the strait gate: for wide is the gate, and broad is the way, that leadeth to destruction, and many there be which go in thereat: because strait is the gate, and narrow is the way, which leadeth unto life, and few there be that find it" (Matt. 7:13, 14).

"For many be called, but few chosen" (Matt. 20:16).

On the basis of such biblical passages (others, however, seem to be more optimistic), Seventh-day Adventists generally have accepted a pessimistic view of the number of the saved. Many feel that the vast majority of people may, for whatever reason, choose not to make a complete surrender to Christ and "enter . . . at the strait gate." Such pessimism does not appear to stop the work of evangelizing, but can actually serve to make it more urgent.

David Koresh took the "few are chosen" texts a step further, however. Although he actively recruited new members for his cult and encouraged his followers to do the same, they did not waste much time on poor prospects.

"Don't cast your pearls before swine," Koresh told Jeff Little when he saw that Jeff's father, Lonnie, was not coming into the fold. Koresh also reportedly told Sherri Jewell to cut all ties to her daughter Kiri after the girl went to live with her father in Michigan.

Koresh may very well have quoted the words of Christ to his followers: "And a man's foes shall be they of his own household. He that loveth father or mother more than me is not worthy of me" (Matt. 10:36, 37).

Although the idea of the "chosen few" can find support in the Bible, Koresh's chosen did not appear to have much sympathy for the "lost," which may account for the fact that some of the lost did not show much sympathy for the Davidians either.

"It's likely that this group was living in a siege mentality and expecting an Armageddon-like battle between themselves—the righteous ones—and the people on the outside," commented Stephen Mann of the University of Texas Health Science Center.

Whatever mentality they were living with, the idea of the chosen few may have been attractive to people Koresh tried to recruit. To be privy to special information, part of a special class, to know things that no one else on earth did, to serve the messiah and usher in the kingdom of God—what more could they want?

6. Boarding academy mentality. With all due respect to boarding academies, those within Adventist circles do have a reputation for proliferating regulations. Rules may be necessary, but some students seem to obey them simply because they exist. They never seem to grasp the concept or reasoning behind the rules. Such rules and regulations remain external, and the principles never get internalized. The same result might happen in an extremely strict home that teaches children only to obey, not to think for themselves.

Once on their own, such children may react in several ways. Some may rebel. Others may continue in the same set of rules from force of habit. Or they may look for some power figure, such as David Koresh, to tell them what to wear, eat, etc., since they never learned to internalize the principles governing these things for themselves.

The nonthinking mentality is not the automatic result of attending a boarding academy or even from growing up in a strict home. Rather it is the result of being told to keep a certain rule or set of rules, and for some reason, never understanding or accepting the principles behind them.

Branch Davidians didn't depend on Koresh just for spiritual guidance. They leaned on him for everything. And he had an opinion on everything, from what they wore to what they ate. When he first became their prophet, Branch Davidians could buy the food and drinks they wanted. Later Koresh forbade any changes in the prescribed diet. As we mentioned earlier, he had one family thrown out of the Palestine camp after a search revealed that, against his wishes, they had bought French fries in town.

"No matter how vital we think the role of leadership in the rise of a mass movement," wrote Eric Hoffer, "there is no doubt that the leader cannot create the conditions which make the rise of a movement possible. He cannot conjure a movement out of the void. There has to be an eagerness to follow and obey, and an intense dissatisfaction with things as they are, before movement and leader can make their appearance. When conditions are not ripe, the potential leader, no matter how gifted, and his holy cause, no matter how potent, remain without a following" *(The True Believer,* p. 103).

In other words, Vernon Howell could not have become David Koresh if he had not been able to find and convince others to follow him.

Men just out of the armed forces make ideal converts for a mass movement, according to Hoffer. They feel "alone and lost in the free-for-all of civilian life. The responsibilities and uncertainties of an autonomous existence weigh and prey upon him. He longs for certitude, camaraderie, freedom from individual responsibility, and a vision of something altogether different from the competitive free society around him" *(ibid.,* p. 48).

Perhaps the Seventh-day Adventist Church should consider the similarities between the rules and regulations that govern young church members during their childhood or while they attend a boarding academy and those controlling an army. Could it be that young Adventists, floundering out in the world for the first time on their own, might be more susceptible to a cult for the same reasons a newly discharged soldier might be?

The greater the frustration, the greater the susceptibility to making a radical change in one's life in an attempt to alleviate that frustration—in other words, the greater the danger of joining a cult.

The routine and safety of Ranch Apocalypse apparently appealed to the desire by some to have their lives simplified, to have someone make their decisions for them. As a result they became the disciples of David Koresh.

Ellen White had some interesting counsel for Seventh-day Adventists on rules and regulations. "Men are not to make rules and regulations for their fellowmen. The Bible has given the rules and regulations that we are to follow. We are to study the Bible, and learn from it the duty of man to his fellow-man. 'The law of the Lord is perfect, converting the soul'" *(General Conference Bulletin,* April 6, 1903).

While advising against numerous rules and regulations, she also came to the defense of certain standards. "Those who are professedly sons and daughters of God should elevate the standard, and have no fellowship with the unruly who would have rules and regulations made to meet the cases of the disobedient. The Sanitarium, unless hedged about with vigilant rules and regulations, would soon become a hotbed of iniquity" *(Medical Ministry,* p. 142).

While Ellen White's defense of rules and then statements against making numerous and excessive regulations might at first glance seem contradictory, it seems she might have been looking for some sort of balance and in the end trying to point others to the reasons behind the rules.

"Instead of toiling to prepare set rules and regulations, you might better be praying and submitting your own will and your ways to Christ. . . . The Lord Jesus loves His heritage, and if men will not think it their special prerogative to prescribe rules for their fellow laborers, but will bring Christ's rules into their life and copy His lessons, then each will be an example, and not a judge" *(Evangelism,* pp. 117, 118).

7. Total embarrassment. Two cult members accepted David Koresh as a prophet and told all their friends and family the same. Their enthusiasm for their new life, family, and friends apparently knew no bounds.

They turned over their paychecks earned outside the compound, which sometimes totaled more than $80,000 a year. In addition, they gave him their life savings, which for some may have amounted to several hundred thousand dollars. Two cult members bought Koresh a house, valued at $350,000, and then tried to take out a $500,000 loan against it for him. Furthermore, they maxed out any credit card they could get their hands on, and payments alone on credit card debt for those two topped $10,000 per month.

Then came the shoot-out. The two cult members expected to die—they had planned on it, and they were committed to Koresh with all their hearts. If they came out, they would face not only mountains of debt but also the incredulity of family members. Rumor had it that a Texas law required execution for anyone killing a Texas lawman. So to their minds they had a choice. On the one hand financial ruin, the embarrassment of failure, deprogramming, and possible execution or a lifetime rotting in jail. All this in addition to the eternal damnation daily threatened by Koresh. Or on the other hand lay sweet release, immediate glory, a planet of their own to populate with a perfect mate, and the end of all trouble.

If you had to choose between the two options above, which would you choose? Death or total embarrassment?

According to cult experts, if cult members follow their leader in committing strange or illegal acts, it becomes more difficult for them to leave the group.

When a person has been so dominated and humiliated, it is very hard to exit. People stay because it's such a big step to admit to themselves and to the world, "I was misled, I was cheated, and I should have left this group years ago."

Jan Keith, vice president of the Cult Awareness Network, had an idea how cult members would answer that question. "They are never going to come out," she predicted before the final fiery blaze. "I don't expect a good ending to this."

Experts in psychology believe that religious sects that believe God's kingdom on earth is imminent may adopt views that make death or suicide easy options. "When a person believes that he or she will live as is until the end of the age, then the fear of death becomes neutralized," said Wayne Oates, author of a religious psychiatry textbook.

Cult members would be unlikely to back out or run away from Koresh's plan to burn the compound, according to another cult expert. "They have come to build their lives around him [Koresh], and whatever he says is right."

8. The appeal of the sinful messiah. The Branch Davidians must have felt frustrated with trying to be good. They tried, in their own strength, to be perfect, and to the surprise of no one but themselves simply couldn't get it right.

David Koresh fixed all that. Especially when it came to the issue of hard rock music. If you were a rock-solid, died-in-the-wool Seventh-day Adventist, would you listen to heavy metal? Probably not. But if you were a Branch Davidian, you could mix rock and religion—keep your heavy metal and rocket to heaven. You could drink beer (on occasion). If you were a woman, you could marry the "Messiah" and bear children who would one day rule the world. And if you were a man, don't worry. Your perfect mate, taken from your rib, would be yours—along with a personal planet.

If you were an Adventist who felt guilty about liking heavy metal music but didn't want to give it up and wanted to have someone tell you that you could listen to Megadeath and still go straight to heaven, Ranch Apocalypse might not have been such a bad place to be.

9. "We're a family." They were old and young, Black and White, all with a shared vision that cut across social lines: mechanic, Harvard-educated lawyer, engineer, computer programmer, real estate salesman, theology student, social worker, musician.

No single thread explains why people of different cultures, different countries, and different generations sacrificed themselves and their children for the preaching of a high school dropout who claimed to be Christ.

"In a way, they were all searching for something," said Rachel Bernstein, coordinator of a cult clinic. "They were looking for someone who had the answer, a belief system to help them make sense of the world. It led them to a man like David Koresh, who promised to offer all the answers, how to interpret their lives."

The compound included some 18 Britons, nine Australians, three Canadians, and an Israeli. At least 15 found their way to Texas through Hawaii.

Six were above age 60, and 30 between 20 and 40. And 17 were children no more than 10 years old. Many had never lived anywhere else.

Experts say that millions of ordinary people have been attracted to such tight-knit groups. Most new members never expect that the groups they are joining could become violent or abusive.

"People think that . . . it's only the dregs of society who get into cults, but that is simply not true," said Margaret Singer, a psychiatrist who has worked with more than 3,000 former cult members. "Almost everybody, at some time, is vulnerable to joining these groups," she went on. "Often it's when people are mildly to moderately depressed. They're in between jobs, or between college and a job, or they've recently been jilted or divorced—then these groups can be appealing to them."

"They often join for good reasons," said Cynthia Kisser, executive director of the Cult Awareness Network. "They think that they are choosing what is a normal church or group of some type. Cults are very deceptive," she added. "They do not tell you what it will really be like for you until you have made friends in the group and develop close affection for members of the group."

According to a collective profile drawn by religious experts, cultists are usually insecure, have low self-esteem, and have suffered tragic events, such as child abuse, neglect, or death in the family.

Even the most bizarre cults cater to perfectly normal needs: for a philosophy that makes the world comprehensible, for security and fellowship, for improving the society in which one lives. Millions of organizations, from churches to self-help groups to political parties, exist in some measure to satisfy some of those needs.

Cult members get recruited by older well-trained cult members who befriend them before introducing them to higher officials in the cult. New members often find themselves attracted to a group's seemingly fresh ideas. Other members make the new recruit feel wanted, and the newcomer gradually comes to distrust the outside world and rely on the group's (and leader's) approval. Typical cult members, who usually have a higher-than-average IQ, then find themselves drawn away from their family and friends.

Potential cult members next receive indoctrination or "an odd interpretation of the Bible from a charismatic leader who is very charming, intelligent, and a little—or a whole lot—disturbed," according to Lynn Mitchell, a University of Houston expert in religious groups.

Mitchell, who has followed cults, said that Koresh and other leaders convince their members that their interpretation of the Bible is true. Eventually, members begin to believe that the world is corrupt, and paranoia sets in.

Phillip Arnold, executive director of the Reunion Institute, said that cult members tend to be idealistic people. They are interested in spiritual things as opposed to materialistic items.

Persons most likely to join a cult would be those in need of a connection, people who have recently been cut loose from their psychological moorings. The classic example is a college student away from home for the first time. Or it might be someone who has just been divorced, lost a job, or undergone a crisis of faith. The more alienated people are, the more likely they are to join a radical fringe group led by an alienated, marginal figure such as David Koresh.

"Once they are into the group, these people really believe that they have found the source of the truth," Arnold remarked. "It's like a very secure blanket. It's a good feeling they have. They feel comfortable."

"Most people join cults voluntarily," said Stuart Wright, a sociologist who has studied cults nationwide. "I found that members willingly gave up most of their own individuality in exchange for the feeling of close-knit belonging they found in these groups."

Some cults do trick people into joining and then use behavior modification to break down their autonomy so they will not leave. All cults offer a reassuring retreat from problems in the outside world.

A cult, experts say, is defined by the power relationships within it. Cult members give up their personal power to a leader who purports to have special, magical knowledge denied to the rest of the world. And once members get absorbed into a cult, it slowly subverts their wills.

Through standard indoctrination techniques—isolation,

deprivation, peer pressure, shaming, secret rituals, forced confession, and vilification of the outside world—the leader and his or her lieutenants convince members that as individuals they are nothing and that the group is everything.

Cult life often consists of sleep and food deprivation, chanting, and preaching to "put you in an altered state," says Betsy Dovydenas, who was a member of Bible Speaks, a Lenox, Massachusetts, religious group, for five years.

Dovydenas, heir to the Dayton-Hudson department store fortune, gave $6.6 million to the group before her husband and parents hired a deprogrammer to get her out.

"It's thought reform," she says. "It's what happens in prison camps."

Once a person has become involved in a cult, however, deprogramming efforts are not very successful. Cult experts estimate their success ratio to be only about 50 percent. Deprogramming works more successfully among members involved for fewer than two years. The less time they've been in, the higher the percentage of success. Little success occurs among people who have belonged to a cult for more than two years.

A cult venerates its leader as the keeper of the "sacred science," the knowledge that only he possesses and that is the path of salvation. In return for surrendering critical judgment and free will, members receive "the feeling that they're making sense of the world and that they have special knowledge that gives them control," said Michael Barkun, a professor of political science at Syracuse University.

"People are often willing to give up freedom for security," according to Lester Kurtz, an associate professor of sociology at the University of Texas.

Cults prey on people's wanting to belong. In that way, cults are like gangs. "Most gang members, especially younger gang members, will talk about gang involvement being the greatest support in their lives, being like family," said Michael Weiss, a clinical psychologist. "They often minimize or don't even think about the criminal aspect." Like gangs, cults often lead people to act in ways they might otherwise think are wrong.

The acts that society considers unthinkable—900 people drinking poison at Jonestown, cult members beating their children to death at the leader's direction—are the result of a thousand tiny steps down the road to personal surrender.

"People in cults often do what the leaders say they should do with their lives rather than what they think they should do with their lives," said another cult expert. "Cults control people's lives."

The unfortunate effect of cult membership, at least for many of the Branch Davidians, was summed up by Berkeley sociology professor Richard Ofshe, who often works with prosecutors in cases of cult crimes.

"Good people can be made to do bad things," he said.

Chapter Nineteen

The Mind Behind the Mania

"I am the son of God," David Koresh, with an air of pomp and circumstance, told his followers. Willingly, they nodded their heads and reverently answered, "Yes, David."

One thing Lonnie Little just couldn't get over when he visited Ranch Apocalypse was the sense of awe that cult members had for David Koresh.

"What was it like, Lonnie?" we asked. "Were the cult members happy? sad? nervous?"

"There was just this sense of 'Wow, we're with God!'" Lonnie replied, describing the worshipful and awe-filled attitude he observed.

◆◆◆

What kind of person was Vernon Howell that he could inspire this type of admiration?

Vernon was a man on a roller coaster, in more ways than one. Sometimes he was ill-kempt, sometimes extremely well-dressed and nice-looking. Sometimes superreligious, sometimes the sinful messiah. Sometimes a would-be rock star, other times afraid to touch a guitar. Sometimes soft-spoken, kind, and mild-mannered, other times haranguing his followers with vulgar and vengeful sermons. Sometimes gentle with children, other times abusive. Sometimes he thought he was Christ, sometimes not.

Eric Hoffer, in *The True Believer,* described the qualities necessary for the successful leader of a mass movement. "The presence of an outstanding leader is indispensable. Without him there will be no movement" (p. 104). Without David Koresh, the Branch Davidians might still be living in Ranch Apocalypse, only it would be called Rodenville and George would be there.

"It needs the iron will, daring, and vision of an exceptional leader to concert and mobilize existing attitudes and impulses into the collective drive of a mass movement. The leader personifies the certitude of the creed and the defiance and grandeur of power. He articulates and justifies the resentment dammed up in the souls of the frustrated. He kindles the vision of a breathtaking future so as to justify the sacrifice of a transitory present" *(ibid.,* p. 105).

Effective leaders of mass movements do not necessarily need exceptional intelligence, noble character, or originality (see *ibid.,* p. 107). The main requirements are: audacity and a joy in defiance, an iron will, a fanatical conviction that he or she is in possession of the one-and-only truth, faith in his or her destiny and luck, a capacity for passionate hatred, contempt for the present, a cunning estimate of human nature, a delight in symbols (spectacles and ceremonials), unbounded brazenness that finds expression in a disregard of consistency and fairness, a recognition that the innermost cravings of a following is for communion and that there can never be too much of it, and a capacity for winning and holding the utmost loyalty of a group of able lieutenants.

A boundless sense of self-confidence is a must in attracting and holding a following. "The quality of ideas seems to play a minor role in mass movement leadership. What counts is the arrogant gesture, the complete disregard of the opinion of others, the singlehanded defiance of the world" *(ibid.,* p. 107).

◆◆◆

To the minds of countless observers, David Koresh possessed most, if not all, of the above. However, it takes more than a leader to forge a mass movement.

Pastor Max Torkelsen II, former pastor of the Diamond Head Seventh-day Adventist Church, said, "My first impression was that he . . . was somehow unbalanced."

From the facts available, others would support that diagnosis. Unbalanced persons actually create a reality within their own minds that becomes the one from which they operate. In other words, unbalanced persons eventually merge their belief(s) or delusions with reality.

As noted earlier in this book, Vernon Howell felt a special affinity for Christ even in his youth, because of the stigma attached to his illegitimate birth. That may have been just the first of many steps toward his later claims to be Christ.

During the next few years Vernon moved from claiming to be a prophet to being King Cyrus to being *a* lamb of God separate from Christ to being *the* Lamb of God. But occasionally, even during his claim to messiahship, he would deny he ever made such statements.

Unbalanced people are aware of all the reality that each of us face, but for some reason they put a different interpretation on it. For Vernon, even the name Mount Carmel may have had a meaning that totally eludes the rest of the world. He may well have compared it to the biblical Mount Carmel, where Elijah met the 400 false prophets and fire rained down from heaven in response to his prayer.

One such example of this type of behavior was the mass murder committed in 1991 in Texas by George Hennard. It appears that Hennard watched the movie *The Fisher King*—at least police found a ticket stub to the movie in his pocket. Rejected by the women in his life, George Hennard saw in the movie a man who had also felt rejected by women. In the movie someone remarked to the rejected one something to the effect of "Why don't you just blow them off?"

George Hennard apparently so identified with the movie that

he walked straight out of there, got a shotgun, and committed the worst mass murder in U.S. history, killing 23 persons and wounding numerous others. He provides an example of the unbalanced behavior some would say also characterized Vernon Howell. George saw himself in *The Fisher King* and went out and did what one of the movie characters said to do. Vernon visualized himself in Revelation and possibly couldn't distinguish between who he was and who he was reading about. In psychosis the mind starts taking on symbolisms, switches back to reality again, then symbolisms, then back to reality. Vernon Howell seemed to be doing the same.

His extreme obsession with the Bible, even from an early age, seemed to build up to his actually wanting to be a part of it. But Vernon may never have seen himself as a prophet if it hadn't been for the theology of the Branch Davidians and the opportunity they presented him.

◆◆◆

Some would like to simplistically villainize Vernon Howell/David Koresh, and certainly the things he did were enough to make most people bristle. Whatever the case, he was incredibly deluded, most likely seriously mentally ill, and yet well enough to sway intelligent people and lead them down the path to long-term mental instability as well.

Despite whatever mental illness he may have had, he was able to sweep through the Diamond Head Adventist Church and form a nucleus for his cult, and then keep most of that nucleus under his continual control right up to the fiery end.

In Hawaii, exposing him to be what he really was seemed nearly impossible once people began to become entrenched in his dogma. People in Hawaii are still shaking their heads and wondering how those who appeared to be intelligent, stable Christians could be attracted to a fanatical leader who preached celibacy and led his followers to an unkempt, disorganized compound, on which the major pieces of furniture consisted of wooden bunk beds nailed to the walls, old rickety chairs, apple crates, and hard wooden benches.

Charles Liu, who followed Max Torkelsen II as pastor of the Diamond Head church, spoke from experience. "Koresh offered a very black-and-white view of life," Liu told one reporter. "He offered something that said, 'Are you tired of thinking, of making decisions in your life? Come to me. I will do the thinking for you. Don't worry anymore.'"

Even men and women of brilliant ability become weary of the myriad decisions that face them in life. Vernon Howell simplified all that. And following him said nothing about their intelligence, although it might have revealed something about their personalities.

"Men of giant intellect are babes in discipline. . . . Men who are content to let others plan and do their thinking for them are not fully developed," wrote Ellen White *(Testimonies,* vol. 3, p. 495).

Research shows that those deceived by mind-control agencies are often sucked into a strange combination of psychology, mysticism, and metaphysics. They are, in fact, mental or emotional adolescents.

Fanatical leaders often draw in victims by preaching in a highly charged manner for a lengthy period of time, such as Koresh did. Emotions are intense, and sometimes the leader appears to produce a drugless high.

Even in his teenage years Koresh would talk about the Bible with literally all who would listen and for as long as they would listen. In a sense, he may have brainwashed himself by the same tactics that he later employed so successfully on his followers.

◆◆◆

Sleep deprivation is another common tactic among cults, and being short on sleep was common among the Branch Davidians.

We asked Lonnie Little how long the average sermon lasted at

Ranch Apocalypse. Although we had heard about the 17-hour marathons, we wondered if that wasn't the exception rather than the rule, with maybe the average being closer to four or five hours.

"Twelve hours is about the average," Lonnie replied, repeating what he had learned not only from his own experience but also from conversations with numerous surviving cult members and families of cult members.

◆◆◆

Psychologists have compared cults to a warm womb to which members want to return for a safer period of life. Not requiring its members to think independently, the groups remove responsibility and worry from the lives of those who belong.

Those who dabble in cultism initially find a group of people who show absolute devotion to each other, such as the young adult group in Hawaii. They have a strong desire to conform, seek a mission in life, and are eager to please. Furthermore, they enjoy the feeling that they are accepted by "the family" that they so desperately desire.

After a short indoctrination period, a person may be confused because of the programmed action, the lack of sleep, the simple, bland food, and the cajolery and other techniques used by cult members to get him or her to stay. The intense activity that goes on constantly leaves little time for contacting family and friends. Many people make decisions to stay with a cult after a period of seemingly endless discourses, activities, and affection from the group.

It takes a unique, charismatic individual to command such allegiance. The human mind is complex, and understanding fanaticism is not always easy. However, Ellen White gave Adventists a profile of fanaticism in her book *Mind, Character, and Personality,* volume 1, pages 38ff. According to her, fanatical persons will demonstrate the following characteristics:

1. They mingle their own particular traits of character with the works of God.

2. They choose their own way, will not listen to counsel, and pervert biblical principles.

3. They work to serve God and self at the same time.

4. They place great emphasis on "excitement of feeling."

5. They get involved in strange procedures.

6. They are naturally combative, and don't care if they harmonize with others or not. They are dictatorial, severe, and antagonistic.

7. They trust to their own righteousness and follow a self-established standard.

Based on our study of thousands of pages detailing the life of David Koresh, we would say he fits every one of the above characteristics.

Incidentally, mingling his own particular traits of character with the works of God would fit right in with our earlier definition of psychosis. One could almost conclude that such persons would not only be considered fanatical by Ellen White, but also be considered clinically mentally ill by today's standards.

◆◆◆

Lonnie Little, whose son Jeff died in the fire, went to Waco several years before the showdown to try to persuade Jeff to leave the cult.

"I drove 22 hours straight to get there," Lonnie said, "and when I got to the compound in the late afternoon, Jeff greeted me warmly. We went into town for a brief time and then returned to the compound, where I was asked to attend Bible study. This lasted way into the night, and by then you can imagine how exhausted I was, having been up now for more than 30 hours."

"But when I observed the abuse of the children," Lonnie continued, "the terrible living conditions, and the strangeness of it all, I made a decision to leave, which I did, without even saying goodbye to Jeff. I never saw him again."

Lonnie Little felt the pull of the cult and understood the

entrapment of mind control. He observed firsthand the frightening psychological coercion used to keep members from leaving the group.

Also he knew that Jeff the cult member was not the same as the Jeff he knew as his son and a member in good and regular standing in the Seventh-day Adventist Church.

Jeff was a victim of mind control. David Koresh taught him to lose faith in himself, other people, and the world. Koresh's influence somehow drew Jeff into a bizarre universe of disillusioned alienation from the everyday world—a universe in which he was taught that God traveled in a special vehicle that took 16 seconds to traverse the distance from earth to heaven.

Koresh encouraged an "end-of-the-world" mentality by quoting Scripture out of context and making personal interpretations and applications. Somehow he led his followers to believe that they could not trust their own minds, and he introduced with this philosophy an element of fear until his converts were afraid to leave.

With all possessions forsaken and turned over to Koresh, the Davidian followers were susceptible to guilt, shame, and dependence upon him for everything they needed. He became their family leader—and their "God."

In *The Great Controversy* we are told: "Many are the ways by which Satan works through human influence to bind his captives. He secures multitudes to himself by attaching them by the silken cords of affection to those who are enemies of the cross of Christ. Whatever this attachment may be, parental, filial, conjugal, or social, the effect is the same; the opposers of truth exert their power to control the conscience, and the souls held under their sway have not sufficient courage or independence to obey their own convictions of duty" (p. 597).

◆◆◆

And what, as noncult members, is our duty?

Each of us must speak against error. We must become educated about fanaticism and know how to avoid it. And we must share that knowledge with others—especially our children.

Ever on the alert, we must guard what goes into our minds and control our habits and affections.

God, through inspiration, counseled us on how to meet fanaticism should we come in contact with it:

1. We must study God's mind and will.

2. We must refuse to enter controversy, but affirm what we know. ("It is written" is to be the test.)

3. We must guard our expressions and attitudes.

4. We must avoid human theories and stay away from controversy over them.

5. We must approach new light carefully, thoughtfully, prayerfully.

6. We must watch and pray.

7. We must ascertain what is the mind of Christ.

8. We must recognize the peril of individual independent attitudes distinct from God's remnant church.

David Koresh destroyed himself and his followers. His tactics to control the minds of his followers caused grief and untold pain to those who still mourn the loss of their loved ones.

It is our hope that the lessons we learn from this tragedy will help build up the church that the Davidians learned to despise.

Chapter Twenty

It Has Happened Before

Isolated and frightened, sustained by weapons and blind faith, members of various cults have died with gruesome regularity during the past few years. Sometimes alone, sometimes by the scores and hundreds, they have died in Jonestown, Guyana, and inner-city Philadelphia. They have died in Washington, Arkansas, and Idaho. And now they have died in Waco, Texas.

Branch Davidians, MOVE, the People's Temple, Aryan Nations—the names and the beliefs have been wildly different, but the fates of those who followed them have been eerily the same.

Some have perished at the hands of law-enforcement officers, others by their own hands before anyone could tear down the small worlds that provided them refuge.

Armed fanatics are nothing new in America. From the Symbionese Liberation Army in 1974 to White supremacist Randy Weaver's shoot-out with federal agents in Idaho in August 1992, the government has been confronted with people willing to die for their beliefs.

Many have recently crossed the line. The antiabortion advocate who gunned down a Florida doctor in cold blood, those who planted a bomb in the New York Trade Center without regard to how many innocent people it would kill, the Serbs who rape, murder, and mutilate in the name of "ethnic cleansing"—all have gone beyond the norms of decency in any culture.

Moved by the power of a charismatic leader, by love of God, by hatred of humanity, and sometimes all of the above, they have died just as so many of them predicted they would, as if there were no other way out.

The following words, sounding all too familiar, might have been penned by David Koresh or Jim Jones. Instead, they came from the lips of avowed racist and Christian fundamentalist Robert Jay Matthews. "It is only logical to assume that my days on this planet are rapidly drawing to a close. I will leave knowing I have made the ultimate sacrifice to secure the future of my children."

Matthews wrote those words not long before he engaged police in a shoot-out near Seattle. He died as he expected. A flare police said they fired to illuminate the area ignited the house where he was hiding. It burned to the ground.

That happened in 1984. A year later in Philadelphia, when members of a tiny cult called MOVE barricaded themselves in a private home, police dropped a bomb on the house, ostensibly to open a hole in the roof for a tear-gas assault. That house and 60 others burned—11 people died.

◆◆◆

Survivalist cult leaders teach followers that they will be persecuted for their faith, much like the Jews at Masada or Jesus Himself.

Like the most fervently loyal believers of the first century, Branch Davidians were unlikely to be aggressors, but they would kill to protect their families and spiritual brothers and sisters.

Unlike Koresh's Branch Davidians, most nonconventional religious groups never make news. They live peacefully in communities across the country. Often neighbors don't even know they're there, cult experts say. "The reason we don't hear about most of them is that most don't have much money and most aren't armed," says J. Gordon Melton, author of *The Encyclopedic Handbook of Cults in America.*

"They're by and large fairly harmless groups," says Richard Stephens, a sociologist at George Washington University. "They're not usually big enough or scary enough to bother anyone."

But cult leaders have the power to gradually push their followers in such a direction, partly by making the outside world appear to be an evil and hostile place.

Jim Jones used that method. He would send some of his men out at night to shoot shotguns and pistols near some of his buildings. Then he would tell his followers that it was their enemies who were going to attack them. He used fear tactics to get his followers to move with him.

Cult leaders claim more and more moral authority, and if it is a religious-based cult, the leader may finally declare that he is the only pipeline to God.

Jones eventually took his congregation to Guyana, where in 1978 more than 900 of his followers committed suicide or were killed.

"There is unfortunately a rise in this sort of fanaticism all across the world," President Bill Clinton remarked during the Waco standoff. "We may have to confront it again."

◆◆◆

The alarming part of the scenario for Seventh-day Adventists is the effect that the actions of such persons could have on religious liberty.

Undoubtedly, careful research into the actual happenings at Waco will reveal that the ATF engaged in not a little bit of show-boating during the initial raid. They had called a number of media personnel and were actually engaged in an attempt to justify their existence and raise their budget. If they could have walked out of the compound with a huge stash of weapons and ammunition and no casualties, the ATF would certainly have gained respect in the public eye.

In addition to their attempts at attracting the media, the

entire raid appeared, in retrospect, to be totally unnecessary. Numerous Waco residents testified to seeing Koresh unwinding on a regular basis at the Chelsea Street Pub and Grill, jogging outside the compound, etc. The entire scenario could have been avoided by nabbing Koresh outside the compound rather than staging a full-scale raid complete with helicopters and news media.

Fringe groups and militants were quick to catch that point. And some of Koresh's supporters were, indeed, frightening characters.

Louis Beam, Jr., an ex-Houston grand dragon of the Ku Klux Klan and who once topped the FBI's 10 Most Wanted List, tried to steal the show one day during the standoff. Beam's former escapades included violent protests against Vietnamese shrimp fishermen along the Gulf Coast. Later he was acquitted of charges of conspiring to overthrow the government.

"I'm being taken to jail for asking the forbidden question!" Beam shouted during his arrest one Thursday for criminal trespass. He had been trying to get into the daily press briefing that he had been evicted from once before.

His question: "Are we becoming a police state?"

The siege drew a hard core of survivalists, White supremacists, and others enraged by what they see as a government assault on a person's home, church, and right to bear arms.

"Wherever we go, these people follow us like a Greek chorus," says Jack Killorin of the ATF.

Another activist, Jeannie Bowman, showed up at a hillock offering a distant view of the compound. She was handing out leaflets—signed "the Common Sense Patrol"—likening the storming of the compound to that of the Alamo in March of 1836.

Future Texans, the pamphlet suggested, will cry, "Remember Mount Carmel!" Said Bowman: "These people have been labeled a cult, but I haven't seen any chicken-chokin' going on."

"This is not unusual" in central Texas, El-Hadi Shabazz said of such don't-tread-on-me-types. Shabazz, who prosecuted cult leader David Koresh in the 1987 shoot-out, observes that "There are more of them than we really think."

The Libertarian Party has demonstrated against the ATF in Dallas and Waco. Followers of the Kingdom Resurrection Ministry of Smithville, Oklahoma, protested on Bowman's hillock.

Members of fringe religious groups have buttonholed reporters wherever they could find them, hoping to spread their messages. Some erected crosses while others prayed.

Ronnie Carter, in camouflage fatigues and a long beard, drove his motorcycle from Big Springs, Texas. He said he was angry because the federal government is hiding its role in attacking the Davidian compound. "They tell you anything and keep it all covered up, like Kennedy's murder. They did the same with Lincoln. I can't prove it, but I know it. Because I talk to God a lot."

Statements like that from persons such as Ronnie Carter make many people cringe.

Brad Douglass, of Amarillo, Texas, certainly wasn't happy about sharing his home state with David Koresh or anyone like him. You can hear it in the guarded way he described himself as a "fundamentalist." To him it means, "I read and believe my Bible and go by it as strictly as I can."

"Waco gives religion a bad name. And the guy who killed the abortion doctor in Florida," Douglass adds, speaking of Michael F. Griffin, charged with murdering Dr. David Gunn. "What kind of image is he giving people who are Christian?"

Certainly not a very attractive one.

◆◆◆

News stories linking people of ardent faith with violent acts—from the United States to the Middle East—reinforce a longstanding bias against anyone loosely labeled "fundamentalist." If the word *cult* is a term to avoid, the label *fundamentalist* might rank close behind it.

A nationwide *U.S.A. Today* Gallup poll of 1,007 adults found that a majority (61 percent) consider fundamentalists to be highly principled and 36 percent view them favorably. However, 57 percent call fundamentalists intolerant and 55 percent label them as extremists.

Fundamentalists themselves join in the criticism. Fifty-two percent of fundamentalists say that they are intolerant, and 48 percent call themselves extremists.

Maude R. Gibson, of Virginia Beach, Virginia, an Episcopalian, sees fundamentalists as "Bible thumpers" who are "not rational and more likely to take their religious views into the political [arena]. They have eccentric mannerisms. They judge others, and that's breaking a commandment."

Social scientists say that *fundamentalist* has become almost synonymous in the press and popular usage with a nasty set of adjectives: "intolerant, nasty, narrow-minded hayseed, poorly educated, and anti-intellectual," says John Green, a political science professor at the University of Akron.

But such stereotyping is easy, lazy, popular—and wrong, Green observes. Fundamentalist has long since slipped its moorings as a title for a specific early twentieth-century Protestant Christian set of beliefs in the inerrant, literal truth of the Bible and the imminent return of Jesus. It has become equated with anyone who has "a very strict view of the tenets of their religious faith. So you can find Catholic fundamentalists or even Jewish fundamentalists even though they may not agree with any of the historic doctrines," Green says.

And, experts say, fundamentalists who fit the original definition may have come by their zealous image honestly, even proudly, as warriors battling secular, materialist values.

George Marsden, a Notre Dame history professor and author of *Understanding Evangelicalism and Fundamentalism,* says, "They don't have illusions about the world in certain ways. They realize there are terrible problems, and only religious faith can deal with it."

Seventh-day Adventists certainly take the Bible seriously and would undoubtedly be classed by some as fundamentalist

Christians. One newspaper article during the siege started out, "Seventh-day Adventists, who take the Ten Commandments literally . . ." as if taking the Ten Commandments literally were something very out of the ordinary.

However, commandments such as "Thou shalt not kill" and "Thou shalt not steal" are all taken literally not only by other Christians, but by the government of our country, which has not only enacted similar laws, but enforces them.

"Religion is a razor's edge," says Ben Andrews of Louisville, Kentucky, who identifies with no denomination but calls himself "very spiritual." "There's no big sign that says 'Oops, you stepped off; you'd better get back on.' And there's the verse that says 'Let him that is without sin cast the first stone.' "

That's the attitude government and many Christians try to take toward other religions.

"You don't want the federal government nosing around in religion. That is dangerous precedent," one religious expert said. Like other religious scholars, he believes that society must tolerate extremes in religion to preserve mainstream faiths, barring evidence of federal crimes. "There have always been unusual and eccentric groups operating in the United States. That results from a nation in which maximum religious liberties are assured."

Several experts on religious cults said that federal authorities were ill-equipped to deal with this siege's risky religious overtones. "The government had no understanding of religious consciousness here, even if it is oddball, sectarian consciousness," said Frank Flinn of Washington University in St. Louis, a researcher on church-state issues and cults.

"To make an assault on the compound just when Koresh was writing about the seven seals of the book of Revelation, obviously on [edge about the end of the world], how could they not know the kind of reaction this would prompt from him?"

Cult researcher Carl Raschke, a professor of religious studies at the University of Denver, said, "I think this is a lesson that law enforcement does not understand the religious mind."

Robert Boston, an official of Americans for Separation of Church and State, had a thought that might have future meaning for many Seventh-day Adventists who believe in an upcoming persecution. "What will occur in three to five weeks when this is all over?" Mr. Boston asked. "There may be calls to crack down on the cults. But a cult can be any group that people don't like."

◆◆◆

The Seventh-day Adventist Church has done much to distance itself from David Koresh, and rightly so. His life and teachings were virtually out of harmony with most everything Seventh-day Adventism stands for.

However, if you take a careful look at the characteristics of a cult, you can understand how Seventh-day Adventists may one day unwillingly bear this label.

Experts say that there are currently somewhere between 600 and 1,500 cults nationwide. A steady growth in cult activity has continued during recent years.

Cults have always been around, but they have really blossomed in the twentieth century. This might be partly because of the development of urban centers and greater freedom to deviate from society within cities. In an urban area, if a person has a kooky idea, he or she is more likely to find six or seven other people who agree.

Like the Branch Davidians, most cults have a powerful, charismatic leader and a flock of devoted followers. Together, they lead alternative lifestyles that leave them largely cut off from the world.

But what makes a cult a cult? They share many characteristics. Cults may exhibit one or all of the following qualities:

1. Cult members are isolated from the outside world and any testing of reality that it could provide.

2. Members are encouraged or required to give up private property.

3. Outsiders are viewed as evil.

4. Members swear total allegiance to an all-powerful leader whom they believe to be in some way superhuman and support the leader's cause, no matter what the effect.

5. Cults are often apocalyptic and believe themselves to be the remnant who will survive the soon-approaching end of the world.

6. Members sometimes stockpile weapons or otherwise prepare for a violent showdown.

7. Unusual sexual relationships and/or physical abuse may occur.

8. Followers are weakened by being forced to depend upon the group to solve problems.

9. The members' existence is only for material survival while at the same time they make false promises to work to improve society.

10. Cults are often anti-woman, anti-child, and anti-family.

◆◆◆

Seventh-day Adventists, like many conservative Christians, would probably prefer to be called practically anything other than that four-letter word *cult.* And they have good reason, considering its current negative connotation. Also, cult characteristics in general simply do not fit any mainline Protestant church, such as the Seventh-day Adventist Church.

For example, stockpiling weapons in preparation for a violent showdown or involvement in unusual sexual relationships or abuse. The Seventh-day Adventist Church encourages its members to live normal, independent lives rather than forcing them to depend upon the group to solve their problems. Of course, they may look to their religion to help them solve life's problems, but that is purely a matter of choice.

The cult characteristic of existence for material survival while making false promises to work to improve society couldn't be further from the example set by the Adventist Church, which has the second-largest parochial school system in the world, in addition to a network of hospitals, colleges, and famine and relief organizations for disaster victims and the poor.

And it would be a far stretch to consider Adventists anti-woman, anti-child, or anti-family. The Seventh-day Adventist Church encourages normal family life, kindness toward children, and has taken an increasingly active role in giving women leadership positions within the church.

Members of the Adventist Church certainly do not swear allegiance to an all-powerful leader with messiahlike status, although a few misguided members may have elevated the writings of Ellen White to a status higher than either she or the church would recommend. Her writings, in the eyes of the church, should lead to further study of and clarify the Scriptures, not take the place of it.

Some would contend that there are Adventists who, like the ancient Jewish Essenes, have, for whatever reason, seen fit to isolate themselves from the outside world and any testing of reality that it could provide. Although this scenario might exist (especially in large Adventist communities where a college or boarding academy is located, or among certain self-supporting institutions), even there such groups make efforts to reach out and be a part of the community. "Ye are the salt of the earth," Jesus said, and Adventists, for the most part, believe this and try to avoid isolationism.

The Adventist Church encourages its members to tithe, which is nothing out of the ordinary for any Christian denomination. It offers no comparison, however, to the level of sacrifice demanded by David Koresh. Tithe is 10 percent of income. Koresh demanded the entire paycheck, maxed his followers' credit cards, emptied their savings accounts, and had them scrambling to take out a home equity loan on the house they bought for him.

Are outsiders considered evil? Yes and no. The Bible teaches that Christ will separate the good from the bad, the sheep from the goats, at His second coming. Although Adventists, like any other Christian group, are to love their neighbors as themselves, some may tend to see those who have not accepted the Adventist lifestyle as somehow less committed. But on reflection they recognize that God is still in control of, and at work in, the rest of the world.

CHAPTER TWENTY-ONE

IT WILL HAPPEN AGAIN

Cults are often apocalyptic and believe themselves to be the remnant that will survive the soon-approaching end of the world. As for that description, Adventism has always had an apocalyptic emphasis.

An interest in the end of time is shared, however, not just by cults, but by a large number of Americans. Experts say that between 30 and 50 percent of Americans believe that Jesus Christ will return to earth and form a heavenly kingdom.

"Fundamentalist preachers . . . have warned us of earth's imminent ending, especially from their television pulpits, for a long time," wrote one newspaper columnist. "They have never, however, declared that they were taking up their last collection, apparently sure that they can take it all with them on the last day" ("Despite Signs Both Far and Near, the Apocalypse Isn't Now," Chicago *Tribune,* Mar. 8, 1993).

"Interest in the millennium and the Advent of Christ is growing exponentially," said Lynn Mitchell, scholar in religious studies at the University of Houston. "We see today millions of Christians studying the Bible for those very reasons."

Bible prophecy has a deep following among Americans, but religion experts contend that most people don't comprehend the raw power of the kind of faith held by cult leader David Koresh.

Although many Christian groups do believe that the end of the world is near, few people read Bible prophecy in personal terms like Koresh did. He claimed to be a messiah who would open the book of seven seals and trigger a final world judgment.

"In the past couple decades, we've had a sharp upsurge in interest in Bible prophecy," said historian Paul Boyer, author of *When Time Shall Be No More.* Boyer continued by pointing out that such seemingly unrelated events as the Israelis gaining control of Jerusalem in 1967, the threat of nuclear war, and shifts in the global economy are among the signs cultists see that indicate—as prophesied in the Bible—that the end is near and Jesus Christ will return.

Public authorities may face no greater challenge than armed, defiant, tight-knit groups that break the law—particularly those who believe that the country is being destroyed or that the end, the apocalypse, the millennium, is near.

"Anything that smacks of confrontation provokes violence," said Syracuse University political scientist Michael Barkin, who has studied such crises. That's because "such individuals maintain that their world will end in some sort of conflagration or battle. When heavily armed authorities move in, they see it as confirmation of their prediction," Barkin pointed out. "Such groups see themselves in confrontation with an evil force. The presumption is that they are in a nonnegotiable situation. They see themselves as participants in a final battle."

One reason given for the current upsurge in cult growth is the approaching of a new millennium—the twenty-first century—intensifying the general expectation that the end of the world is nearing. Cult experts note that the year 2000 will mark the end of the second millennium—the second 1,000-year period since the beginning of the Christian calendar and a moment of great portent for those who believe in the millennial theory of Jesus' return.

"There possibly are going to be more and more of these kinds of scenarios," commented James Oho, an Idaho sociologist.

But most people who expect the end of the world don't arm themselves or initiate violence.

Other experts suggest that trouble can surface when cult leaders feel that they must defend themselves and their followers against challenges from conventional society. For instance, Koresh may have felt that the authorities were threatening his cult's way of life. And once he decided to challenge authority with weapons, cult experts say that they're not surprised that his followers went along and started shooting.

"It's hard to say these people are a threat to society," Boyer said. "Even in Waco, from their point of view, they fired back in self-defense when satanic government attacked."

Experts in Houston said the fire that sparked the end for David Koresh and his followers doesn't mean that apocalyptic religious sects are violence or suicide prone.

"Most apocalyptic sects do not end in suicide," said William Martin, a Rice University sociologist and religion scholar. "This might play off Jim Jones, for all we know. If Jim Jones didn't do what he did, maybe then David Koresh wouldn't have done what he did."

Said Martin of Koresh, "This guy doesn't represent a movement or a trend."

Dying for a deeply held religious belief is rather common, nonetheless, and David Koresh had totally convinced his faithful that his was the only way to salvation. To their way of thinking, his answer was the only truth that mattered in their lives. They were committed to the death and proved it in that last conflagration.

◆◆◆

We have all tried to make sense of this mind-shattering event. The heredity, childhood, and environment that took an eager Bible-quoting Vernon Howell and transformed him into the dominating David Koresh will continue to undergo examination and analysis in efforts to try to understand the incomprehensible. The primary question, however, will probably remain unanswered: How does an otherwise perfectly rational person become so entrenched in "the cause" that he or she crosses the line of rational thought?

The people in the Mount Carmel compound, with notable exception of Koresh himself, were not uneducated. A Waco lawyer died in the flames. Others were college graduates and lovely young ladies who could have been the girl next door, except that David Koresh bedded them down and impregnated them at his will—all in the guise of his holy duty.

Only one element appears to be a constant in all these outrageous acts. That is the need to have the magic answer that will solve the world's problems—to be absolutely correct. And more important, to reject totally anyone who questions or disagrees or finds fault with that answer. Only a closed mind will take a strong belief and run it to the outer limits of fanaticism. Only then can bloody and unspeakable acts be rationalized.

The key in avoiding becoming involved in a cult yourself is to know their features and head in the opposite direction when even approached by a cultlike organization.

Dividing the world into a "we versus them" mentality has inherent dangers. There are many "types" of people today—liberals and conservatives, Blacks and Whites, pro-lifers and pro-choicers, Republicans and Democrats, straights and gays. Each group has a particular point of view, and each has its own version of the truth.

The problem might arise when we block out hearing anything but our truth and claim that our reality is the only one worthy of consideration. We tend to develop a vocabulary that eliminates any other possibilities.

Whether it is from intellectual laziness or our modern propensity for quick-and-easy solutions to complex problems, we seize upon one good approach as the only good answer to issues that require much more. The resulting attitude can be heard in such expressions as "You people . . ." or "They always . . ." or

"They never . . ." or "Why don't they . . . ?" Carried to its ultimate end, the "we versus them" mentality produced the horror at Mount Carmel.

Those of us who feel tempted to declare ourselves absolutely, unswervingly, brilliantly right about any issue, or who close our ears and minds to what another person believes, or who respond with arrogance toward "them," should remember the babies who died at Mount Carmel on a windy April day. The blindness of the persons responsible for protecting them was complete. Convinced that they were absolutely correct in their beliefs, they carried that attitude to its ultimate and unfortunate conclusion, and their children will never have that choice for themselves.

In addition to avoiding rigidity and knowing the characteristics of a cult, we as individuals must learn to think for ourselves.

Elizabeth Clare Prophet, herself a leader of an organization accused of being a cult, acknowledged that there are plenty of people out there waiting to be plucked by preachers: "They will put on me the responsibility of telling them what to do," she said, adding that she refused to take that responsibility.

"People are by nature idolaters," she went on. "If you let them, they will abdicate their own conscience, their own mind, their own free will."

◆◆◆

Perhaps here we find the real lessons of Waco—to think for ourselves, to guard the avenues to the soul, and to raise children who know how to recognize and then say no to a cult.

CHAPTER TWENTY-TWO

THOSE MAGNETIC MASS MOVEMENTS

Lonnie Little was tired. He was confused. Most of all, he was frustrated. Lonnie's son Jeff didn't want to leave David Koresh. And for his own safety, Lonnie knew that he himself could not endure or withstand cult efforts to draw him in any longer. Already he had a spot picked out at Ranch Apocalypse—a spot where he could park his camper and live. And he knew one thing. If he didn't want to join the cult, he had to leave . . . and leave right away!

Fortunately for Lonnie, that's exactly what he did.

◆◆◆

It seems a mystery to many how someone could be drawn so completely to the Branch Davidians or any similar organization. But the power of "mass movements," as Eric Hoffer calls them, he wonderfully explained in his thought-provoking book *The True Believer.*

Hoffer, an avid reader and student of history as well as of human nature, drew some interesting conclusions about what type of people get drawn to mass movements, why they are attracted, and what it takes to keep such a movement going.

Hoffer's analysis can be quite disturbing for the Christian.

However, while most Christians would not agree with some of the categorizations in Hoffer's book, many of his ideas seem to offer valid insights into what happened at Ranch Apocalypse.

According to Hoffer, persons experiencing some degree of success and fulfillment in their current existence generally will not look for change or join some sort of mass movement. Persons who feel fulfilled usually perceive that they live in a good world, and so they wish to keep the status quo. On the other hand, the frustrated are most likely to favor radical change.

Lonnie Little might not have known it at the time, but his very frustration at not being able to extricate Jeff from cult life may very well have contributed to the "pull of the cult."

The more frustrated people are, Hoffer contends, the more likely it is that they will attempt radical change *(The True Believer,* p. 16).

"If anything ail a man, so that he does not perform his functions . . . he forthwith sets about reforming—the world" (Henry David Thoreau).

According to Hoffer, history is often played out by a combination of superior individuals and the dregs of society *(The True Believer,* p. 29). Superior individuals achieve a large role in the shaping of a movement by virtue of their intellect, talent, or achievement. Individuals at the other extreme, however—the failures, misfits, criminals, outcasts, etc.—also usually have a much larger role than the majority in the middle. This is because the "inferior elements" of a nation are "wholly without reverence toward the present." In their view, "their lives . . . [are] spoiled beyond remedy, and they are ready to waste and wreck" them if necessary in pursuit of some larger dream *(ibid.,* p. 30).

Hoffer pointed out that in many cases the "dregs and malcontents" of Europe populated America and the rest of the New World *(ibid.).* Indeed, frustrated persons can be found in all walks of life, but they frequently appear among the poor, misfits and outcasts, minorities, teenagers, or the overly ambitious.

Additional categories from which Hoffer contends that the

frustrated arise might have special interest for the Christian world. They include those in the grip of some vice or obsession, the mentally unbalanced, the inordinately selfish, bored, or guilty *(ibid.)*.

Persons who experience this degree of frustration have most likely lost faith in themselves. "The less justified a man is in claiming excellence for his own self, the more ready is he to claim all excellence for his nation, his religion, his race, or his holy cause" *(ibid.,* p. 23).

In other words, fanatical racism or religious or patriotic fervor may be an effort by the people to forget their unacceptable selves in the pursuit of some high and worthy cause. If people's individual interests and prospects do not seem worth living for, such persons frantically need something to live for apart from themselves. Hoffer claims that "all forms of dedication, devotion, loyalty, and self-surrender are in essence a desperate clinging to something which might give worth and meaning to our futile, spoiled lives. Hence the embracing of a substitute will necessarily be passionate and extreme" *(ibid.,* p. 24).

The characterization of a frustrated individual seems to fit at least some of the Branch Davidians. Marc Breault and Steve Schneider shared disappointment in not receiving their hoped-for calls to the ministry. David Koresh felt frustration as a result of the rejection he experienced in his childhood, and also because of his failure to convince Jim Gilley and the Tyler Seventh-day Adventist Church of his prophetic status. Sherri Jewell no doubt felt frustrated about her broken marriage.

In addition to frustrations in their personal lives, cult members may have felt frustrated over their own inability to live up to standards they had set for themselves. Cult members, even before their indoctrination, tended to be idealists. They expected great things, and they were disappointed if they could not meet their own expectations.

Perhaps the group of young Adventists in Hawaii, being idealists, were looking for some higher challenge than what they found in their own denomination. Perhaps they wanted a cause that they could live and die for—now. For whatever reason, it seems that they did not see it in mainstream Adventism.

◆◆◆

Once cult members joined the Davidians, their frustrations were not entirely over. However, these frustrations were somehow treated differently than those that had driven them to the cult in the first place. At first glance, one might wonder why they did not consider a second radical change and leave the Branch Davidians. According to Hoffer, "those who are awed by their surroundings do not think of change, no matter how miserable their condition" *(ibid.,* p. 17).

And cult members were definitely in awe of their surroundings, and especially of David Koresh. That was the biggest feeling Lonnie Little remembered about the compound. Everyone reflected a feeling of "Wow! I'm in the presence of God!"

Although Lonnie described the compound as being messy and unkempt, with scanty and unpalatable food, a pervading sense of awe filled it, making it difficult for cult members to realize their true situation.

◆◆◆

Cult members arose at sunup each morning, worked hard until 3:00 p.m., and then listened to sermons that averaged 10 to 12 hours long. Then they collapsed into bed and tried to catch a few hours' sleep before facing the next routine marathon.

In essence, they were kept too busy eking out their own personal existence to even consider a change.

"Where people toil from sunrise to sunset for a bare living, they nurse no grievances and dream no dreams" *(ibid.,* p. 33). "The poor on the borderline of starvation live purposeful lives. To be engaged in a desperate struggle for food and shelter is to be wholly free from a sense of futility. The goals are concrete and immediate. Every meal is a fulfillment; to go to sleep on a full stomach is a triumph; and every windfall a miracle" *(ibid.,* p. 32).

◆◆◆

Evidently some persons find themselves driven by their frustrations to seek some sort of protection from the decisions that they face in daily living, and they see it in the simple life of a cult, because "freedom of choice places the whole blame of failure on the . . . individual" *(ibid.,* p. 35).

"Unless a man has the talents to make something of himself, freedom is an irksome burden. Of what avail is freedom to choose if the self be ineffectual? We join a mass movement to escape individual responsibility, or, in the words of the ardent young Nazi, 'to be free from freedom.' It was not sheer hypocrisy when the rank-and-file Nazis declared themselves not guilty of all the enormities they had committed. They considered themselves cheated and maligned when made to shoulder responsibility for obeying orders. Had they not joined the Nazi movement in order to be free from responsibility?" *(ibid.,* pp. 35, 36).

"Fanatics," said French philosopher Joseph Ernest Renan in 1880, "fear liberty more than they fear persecution."

Any rising movement offers a certain sense of freedom despite the fact that those involved adhere to a strict set of rules and commands. "This sense of liberation comes from having escaped the burdens, fears, and hopelessness" of an unhappy personal life *(ibid.,* p. 36). Escape into a fanatical movement, or in the case of the Davidians, a cult, provides a feeling of deliverance and redemption *(ibid.,* pp. 36, 37).

◆◆◆

Some of the most active members of mass movements, according to Hoffer, are "those who because of a lack of talent or some irreparable defect in body or mind cannot do the one thing for which their whole being craves. No achievement, however spectacular, in other fields can give them a sense of fulfillment. Whatever they undertake becomes a passionate pursuit; but they never arrive, never pause. They demonstrate the fact that we can never have enough of that which we really do not want, and that we run fastest and farthest when we run from ourselves" *(ibid.,* p. 50).

Such persons find "salvation" only by completely forgetting about themselves, and they usually find it in some sort of collective mass movement *(ibid.).* "By renouncing individual will, judgment and ambition, and dedicating all their powers to the service of an eternal cause, they are at last lifted off the endless treadmill which can never lead them to fulfillment" *(ibid.).*

Hoffer's concepts here pose a serious challenge to the Christian. After all, Christians see Christ and the salvation He offers as the only remedy for what ails all of us, and Christians regard all people as possessing some type of "irreparable defect in body or mind," otherwise known as a sinful nature.

The problem might lie in the fact that persons are trying to fill the "God-shaped vacuum" within their souls with something other than God. Or possibly that through some fanatical addiction to even a good religion, they are attempting to earn their way to heaven.

Those who renounce individual will, judgment, and ambition, and dedicate all their powers to the service of an "eternal" cause other than that of Christ, may be temporarily lifted off the endless treadmill that can never lead them to fulfillment. But there is only one truly eternal cause, and it is the cause of the One who has the power to resurrect and destroy, and to give His followers eternal life. "I am he that liveth, and was dead; and, behold, I am alive for evermore, Amen; and have the keys of hell and of death" (Rev. 1:18).

◆◆◆

According to Hoffer, people "who rush into undertakings of vast change usually feel they are in possession of some irresistible power." That power they often find in their new teachings or doctrines. Leaders of the "French Revolution had an extravagant conception of the omnipotence of man's reason and the boundless range of his intelligence. . . . Lenin and the Bolsheviks . . . had blind faith in the omnipotence of Marxist doctrine" *(ibid.,* p. 17). German Nazis experienced an electrifying faith in Adolf Hitler and an overwhelming conviction in their new technique *(ibid.,* pp. 17, 18). David Koresh and the Branch Davidians shared what was for them a life-changing conviction in the secret of the seven seals and the power of Koresh as prophet and messiah.

◆◆◆

An exaggerated self-confidence, combined with a thirst for change and some degree of power, often leads to implementation of change or at least some attempt in that direction. But the final kindling factor necessary to the creation of any mass movement, according to Hoffer, is what he calls "extravagant hope."

"Those who would transform a nation or the world cannot do so by breeding . . . discontent. . . . They must know how to kindle and fan an extravagant hope. It matters not whether it be hope of a heavenly kingdom, of heaven on earth, of plunder and untold riches, of fabulous achievement or world dominion" *(ibid.,* p. 18). Those who transform a nation or the world will not succeed "because they know how to stir up discontent or how to infect people with hatred, but because they know how to preach hope" *(ibid.,* p. 19).

Life was certainly full of hope for the followers of David Koresh—hope, not for this present life, but for a glorious future. A future in which each man would have his own planet and a perfect wife taken from his own rib. A world that sounded somehow better than the heaven in the Bible. A world in which God travels in a spaceship known as a *merkabah* (a term from Jewish mysticism). A world in which only the faithful Branch Davidians who know the meaning of the seven seals can enter.

◆◆◆

One personality trait that Hoffer saw in leaders of mass movements was an inordinate amount of selfishness. "The more selfish a person, the more poignant his disappointments. It is the inordinately selfish, therefore, who are likely to be the most persuasive champions of selflessness" *(ibid.,* p. 51).

That description might never have applied to the followers of David Koresh, but it certainly did to their leader. In his article "Lessons From Waco," Adventist sociologist Caleb Rosado identified the "common denominator" among Koresh's "obsession with the seven seals and the belief that he alone could open them," his "centralizing of possessions and controlling of the money," his "obsession with graphic, promiscuous sex that he alone could engage in," and his "obsession with guns and high-powered weapons." The common denominator in all the obsessions could be summed up in one word—*power (Ministry,* July 1993, p. 9). David Koresh wanted an inordinate amount of power, for himself and himself only.

In the pursuit of that power, he became, to use Hoffer's description, "the most persuasive champion of selflessness"—selflessness for his followers but inordinate selfishness for himself.

In the words of Dr. Rosado: "The charred corpses of an estimated 86 men, women, and children bore grisly testimony that the most seductive force in the world is power. It is the one thing human beings crave most, and in order to possess it the most heinous crimes are committed. While Koresh's departure in a blaze of self-inflicted glory may not have been his preferred climax to the siege, it did allow him to control the final outcome. He took the lust for power to its ultimate limit" *(ibid.,* p. 10).

◆◆◆

Ambitious but frustrated persons who see "unlimited opportunities" are another category of persons whom Hoffer sees as likely to throw themselves into some sort of mass movement. When opportunities appear unlimited, these persons tend to place little value on the present. They have an attitude of "all that I am doing or possibly can do is chicken feed compared with what is left undone" *(The True Believer,* pp. 51, 52).

David Koresh saw his first opportunity in the apparent vacuum of leadership among the Branch Davidians, and he moved quickly to fill it. His belief that he would be involved in greater and greater things reverberated through his statements that the military operation the Davidians were soon to engage in would "make the Los Angeles riots in the aftermath of the Rodney King trial pale in comparison." They were chicken feed.

◆◆◆

Even more important than the doctrine and promises of a mass movement is the refuge it offers from the anxieties, barrenness, and meaninglessness of an individual existence. Group members do away with their own sense of inadequacy by becoming enfolded and absorbed into the closely knit group *(ibid.,* p. 52).

According to Hoffer, effective leaders of mass movements often dwell on the glorious past and the even better future. As for the present, it might be somewhat intolerable (see *ibid.,* pp. 66, 67).

David Koresh spent much time on the glorious past—preaching the perfection and beauty of character of the early church in such a way as to let his followers know that they could never measure up.

A strong indication of the Branch Davidian attitude toward the present appears in what Sherri Jewell said in response to a friend who asked if the Davidians planned to commit suicide. "It's only flesh," she had replied.

Separated by sex and age, crammed into communal bunk-bed rooms without heat, air conditioning, or running water—the Branch Davidian "present" could not have been less inviting. But it fit the plans of David Koresh, and it also fits the picture drawn of mass movements and those who engage in them.

"Faith in the future renders us receptive to change," wrote Hoffer *(ibid.,* p. 19).

Some of Koresh's followers experienced a major change in standard of living to follow their leader. They deserted comfortable homes and hefty incomes to follow their faith in the future.

For those who, like David Koresh, are driven for whatever reason to try to change the world, whether or not they wreck the present life of their followers is totally irrelevant.

"It does not seem to make any difference who it is that is seized with a wild hope—whether it be an enthusiastic intellectual, a land-hungry farmer, a get-rich-quick speculator, a sober merchant or industrialist, a plain workingman or a noble lord—they all proceed recklessly with the present, wreck it if necessary, and create a new world" *(ibid.).*

◆◆◆

The Industrial Revolution serves as one example of a mass movement whose potential, according to Hoffer, "set the minds of manufacturers and merchants on fire." The resulting revolution was as extreme and radical as any religious reformation that ever took place, and in a relatively short time changed the manner of life in England forever *(ibid.,* p. 20).

Under the leadership of David Koresh, in a relatively short time, the lives of his followers changed forever. Marriages split, homes were sold, jobs were given up, and family ties were severed.

Before their conversion most Branch Davidians had little or no idea where their new faith would lead them. Even the actual physical condition and setting of Ranch Apocalypse came as a rude shock to many new arrivals. And what had at first appeared to be a deeper understanding and extension of beliefs that they already held, in the end actually undermined formerly deeply held beliefs regarding the sanctity of marriage, nonviolent behavior, and kindness toward children.

This would have been no surprise to Hoffer, who observed in the early 1950s that "there is often a monstrous incongruity between the hopes, however noble and tender, and the action which follows them. It is as if ivied maidens and garlanded youths were to herald the four horsemen of the apocalypse" *(ibid.)*.

◆◆◆

Because when individuals join a mass movement or similar group they hope to find "change and a chance for a new beginning," they are often open to the idea of a physical move. Migration of the group often serves as a way to promote solidarity and strengthen the group *(ibid.,* pp. 28, 29).

God Himself seems to have used migration for this very purpose. Abraham left his home at God's request, and the children of Israel traveled to Egypt and then back to the Promised Land as a result of God's leading, before being taken as captives to Babylon.

David Koresh must have sensed the power and importance of migration in solidifying his power and leadership, because he encouraged and even demanded it of his followers. Whether from Australia, Hawaii, or England, all must gather at the Ranch Apocalypse and "sit at the feet of the lamb."

"Every mass movement is in a sense a migration—a movement toward a promised land," wrote Hoffer, "and, when feasible and expedient, an actual migration takes place. This happened in the case of the Puritans, Anabaptists, Mormons, Dukhobors, and Zionists. Migration, in the mass, strengthens the spirit and unity of a movement; and whether in the form of a foreign conquest, crusade, pilgrimage or settlement of new land it is practiced by most active mass movements" *(ibid.)*.

Ellen White in her writings has discouraged Seventh-day Adventists from congregating in one place, though certain communities are necessary to maintain and staff educational and healing institutions. Although Jesus was referring to salt that had lost its flavor when He said "ye are the salt of the earth" (Matt.

5:13), one might deduce that too much salt in one city would not be a good thing.

"The instruction is still being given," wrote Ellen White. "'Move out of the cities. Establish your sanitariums, your schools, and offices away from the centers of population.' Many now will plead to remain in the cities, but the time will come erelong when all who wish to avoid the sights and sounds of evil will move into the country; for wickedness and corruption will increase to such a degree that the very atmosphere of the cities will seem to be polluted" *(Selected Messages,* book 2, p. 357).

We might consider Ellen White's counsel for Seventh-day Adventists to move from city to country a migration of sorts. However, since "the country" could be any one of a number of places, it would hardly have a unifying effect in terms of a mass movement. For Seventh-day Adventists and most other Christians, the next expected migration will be a heavenly one.

For the Davidians, however, migrations were underway and attributed to God's leading long before David Koresh came on the scene. Victor Houteff led his faithful first from California to Texas. Houteff and later Davidian prophets predicted a mass migration to the Holy Land at various times. However, it never materialized. David Koresh visited Israel, with the expectation of possibly starting a holy war there himself, which would bring about the end of all things. Since those plans did not materialize, he contented himself with requiring the faithful to migrate to the promised land in Texas. Periodically during Koresh's leadership, a group of select Davidians would "migrate" to their home in California, then back again.

It seems likely that such migrations were more than mere tactical moves. They offered a way of uniting and controlling the group, severing family ties, and solidifying David Koresh's leadership.

◆◆◆

Another method used by some mass movements to solidify

themselves is to disregard family ties. Many rising mass movements have shown a considerable disregard for the family unit. Hoffer believed that a "proselytizing mass movement must break down all existing group ties if it is to win a considerable following" *(The True Believer,* p. 39).

In the case of David Koresh, he split up husbands and wives, taking the wives for himself. Jealousy and petty maneuvering then prevailed among the wives, and thus destroying family units weakened resistance to cult initiatives.

Hoffer, who, one might guess, did not look with extreme favor on Christian values, pointed to statements by Christ about setting a man at variance with those of his own household. To justify his opinion that Christianity wrecked homes and showed disregard for the family, he also referred to Jesus' statement that His disciples were His family.

However, it is worth noting that Koresh and many destructive mass movements separated families as a matter of course and as part of their indoctrination program. In the case of Christianity, a living experience with Christ actually strengthens homes. At times, though, especially during periods of persecution, the strength and incompatibility of convictions held by family members may lead to splitting the family unit. This was not, however, Christ's wish. It was more a by-product of the overall "great controversy," showing itself in a smaller way within family units where some were believers and some were not.

◆◆◆

Sheer boredom also plays a role in driving the growth of mass movements. An individual is "free of boredom only when he is engaged either in creative work or some absorbing occupation or when he is wholly engrossed in the struggle for existence. . . . Where people live autonomous lives and are not badly off, yet are without abilities or opportunities for creative work or useful action, there is no telling to what desperate and fantastic shifts they might resort in order to give meaning and purpose to their lives" *(ibid.,* p. 54).

◆◆◆

Another category of person Hoffer saw attracted to mass movements was that of the sinner. "Fervent . . . religious . . . enthusiasm," he claimed, "often serves as a refuge from a guilty conscience. It is a strange thing that both the injurer and the injured, the sinner and he who is sinned against, should find in the mass movement an escape from a blemished life. Remorse and a sense of grievance seem to drive people in the same direction" *(ibid.,* p. 55).

Could it be that the act of making the ultimate sacrifice, a total self-surrender to the movement of their choice, is for some persons an attempt at atonement? Could it be that burdened down with guilt, perhaps with many rules and lacking the moral maturity to obey those rules for the right reasons, the frustrated throw themselves into some expedient cause with an unhealthy vigor? It seems sad but possible, even plausible, that relentless guilt and a desire to be purged from sin drove some sincere and honest searchers into the inferno at Waco.

Koresh himself suffered under an extreme weight of guilt even during his childhood. Both his mother and grandmother remembered instances of his kneeling by his bed, praying and crying for hours. Perhaps because he had felt such rejection by any potential father figures in his own life, he felt it difficult to receive God's acceptance and forgiveness.

This Jonathan Edwards' "sinners-in-the-hands-of-an-angry-God" mentality is a little too close to the minds of most Christians. Yet God housed even the Ten Commandments in the mercy seat.

"I will sing of mercy and judgment: unto thee, O Lord, will I sing" (Psalm 101:1).

King David might not have been singing about the judgment

if he trembled in terror during every church service, as our Puritan forebears did.

The followers of David Koresh knew the terror of the judgment, and sacrificed accordingly to achieve salvation. Did they have the vaguest idea, especially at the end, what a merciful God would be like? It doesn't seem likely, not with Koresh thundering hellfire and brimstone upon anyone who dared leave the cult.

Lonnie Little, who lost his son Jeff in the blaze, said that if he had learned one thing from his bitter experience that he could share with the world, it would be this: "We are saved by grace."

It's simple. It's for sure. And it was a major pillar of the Protestant Reformation.

Nonetheless cult members gave their bodies, their wives, their money, and finally their lives in an effort to atone for the massive sense of guilt that the Davidians first used to recruit them. Koresh then drove guilt deeper and deeper into their minds every day. Sadly, the sacrifice they made was one God never required.

According to Eric Hoffer, mass movements derive much of their strength and propensity for united action through the self-sacrifice of believers. It has been true not only of the Branch Davidians, but of the Christian church as a whole.

If God owns the cattle on a thousand hills, He could have funded the evangelization of the world and sent angels to do it. But He chose to ask Christians to sacrifice, as He sacrificed for them.

Some have given the ultimate sacrifice and been martyrs for the Christian faith, and others are sure to follow.

David Koresh saw the power of sacrifice in binding others to his personal cause. One potential recruit remembers Koresh asking him, "Are you willing to die for God?"

The young man answered in the affirmative.

"Are you willing to kill for God?" Koresh continued.

The young man thought for a moment, then voiced his uncertainty.

"You just brought me another weak Christian!" Koresh complained to the person who had been recruiting the young man.

Mass movement leaders who foster a readiness to fight and die utilize several techniques to instill a spirit of fearless fervor into their followers.

One way to prepare devotees for the ultimate sacrifice is to strip them of their "individual identity and distinctness." This is done by completely assimilating "the individual into a collective body"—the organization *(ibid.,* p. 60).

In the case of the Branch Davidians, cult members had "no purpose, worth, and destiny apart from" their membership in the cult (*ibid.*). And in order for such assimilation to be effective, it must be thorough. The "joys and sorrows, . . . pride and confidence must spring from the fortunes and capacities of the group" *(ibid.,* p. 61).

"Above all, he [the individual] must never feel alone," wrote Hoffer. "Though stranded on a desert island, he must still feel that he is under the eyes of the group. To be cast out from the group should be equivalent to being cut off from life" *(ibid.)*.

In the case of the Branch Davidians, David Koresh and his knowledge of the seven seals was the only way they saw to salvation. His status as their "God" gave them the feeling that they were always under the eyes of the cult. And to be cut off from the doctrine of the seven seals and the "lamb" who could open them would be, to their minds, the equivalent of eternal death.

Cult members found strength in being part of something "mighty, glorious, and indestructible." Faith for them was "a process of identification." They ceased to be only themselves and became "part of something eternal" *(ibid.,* p. 62).

◆◆◆

"Dying or killing seem easy when they are part of a ritual, ceremonial, dramatic performance or game," wrote Hoffer. "It is one of the main tasks of a real leader to mask the grim reality of dying and killing by evoking in his followers the illusion that they are participating in a grandiose spectacle, a solemn or lighthearted dramatic performance" *(ibid.,* p. 64).

Armies utilize "flags, emblems, parades, music, and elaborate . . . ritual . . . to separate the soldier from his flesh-and-blood self and mask the overwhelming reality of life and death" *(ibid.,* p. 65).

David Koresh used black pajama-type uniforms, a Passover supper, a Star of David flag, and violent Vietnam war movies to toughen his troops and separate them from the true reality of their situation.

"In the practice of mass movements, make-believe plays perhaps a more enduring role than any other factor. . . . There is no doubt that in staging its processions, parades, rituals, and ceremonials, a mass movement touches a responsive chord in every heart. Even the most sober-minded are carried away by the sight of an impressive mass spectacle" *(ibid.,* pp. 65, 66).

According to Ellen White, the Jewish nation might have received Christ differently if He had been willing to rely on a little more showmanship and a little less truth. "When Christ came to this world, men did not recognize His divine character, or realize the nature of His mission. If He had come with pomp and ceremony, to reign as a temporal prince on the throne of Jerusalem, the whole Jewish nation would have acknowledged Him as the Messiah" *(Signs of the Times,* July 8, 1889).

◆◆◆

Leaders often rely on such "mass spectacles" to deaden in their followers the pain of the present. In a mass movement, wrote Hoffer, "the people called upon to attack the past in order to liberate the present must be willing to give up enthusiastically any chance of ever tasting or inheriting the present. . . . Hence the inevitable shift in emphasis once the movement starts rolling. The present—the original objective—is shoved off the stage and its place taken by posterity—the future. More still: the present is driven back as if it were an unclean thing and lumped with the detested past. The battle line is now drawn between things that are and have been, and the things that are not yet.

"To lose one's life is but to lose the present; and, clearly, to lose a defiled, worthless present is not to lose much" *(The True Believer,* p. 66).

For the Branch Davidians, the present represented "a mean preliminary to a glorious future; a mere doormat on the threshold of the millennium." This current world was "a place of exile, a vale of tears leading to the heavenly kingdom" *(ibid.,* p. 67).

Most Christian faiths share the attitude to some degree. "This world is not my home, I'm just a'passing through" are the words on many lips, especially during times of difficulty. Few carry the deprecation of the present to such extremes, however, as did the Branch Davidians.

◆◆◆

When Lonnie Little visited the compound, all cult members shared one bathroom in which they flushed the toilet with a bucket of water but once every three hours. They had to carry the water from a mile away. Cult members rose at sunup, worked hard all day, fasted often, and exercised rigorously. Having given their all to Koresh, their eyes were clearly fastened to the future.

"When everything is ahead and yet to come," wrote Hoffer, "we find it easy to share all we have and to forego [sic] advantages within our grasp" *(ibid.,* p. 68).

Frustrated individuals receive a sense of "enormous joy" from deprecating the present. Perhaps they do so because by expounding on the "baseness and vileness of the times," they "soften their feeling of failure and isolation." According to Hoffer, they are saying, "'Not only our blemished selves, but the lives of all our contemporaries, even the most happy and successful, are worthless and wasted'" *(ibid.,* p. 72).

"Dreams, visions and wild hopes are mighty weapons and realistic tools" *(ibid.,* p. 73).

David Koresh certainly knew how to harness the power of such powerful psychological tools and to use them to his advantage.

◆◆◆

Glorifying the past is another means of minimizing the pain of the present. "There is no more potent dwarfing of the present than by viewing it as a mere link between a glorious past and a glorious future," wrote Hoffer *(ibid.,* p. 69). "It makes the present seem as a section in a procession or a parade. The followers . . . see themselves on the march with drums beating and colors flying. They are participants in a soul-stirring drama played to a vast audience" *(ibid.).*

◆◆◆

In order to motivate the faithful, leaders of a mass movement must place before their followers some "ultimate and absolute truth" and the idea "that there is no truth or certitude outside" their own *(ibid.,* p. 75). The sureness of any such doctrine is more important than its meaning. Even a profound and sublime doctrine will be ineffective, "unless it is presented as . . . the one and only truth" *(ibid.,* p. 76).

In order for this doctrine to be effective, it must not be totally understood, only believed in. "We can be absolutely certain only about things we do not understand," wrote Hoffer. "A doctrine that is understood is shorn of its strength" *(ibid.).*

Among Koresh's disciples at Ranch Apocalypse, one thing stood absolute: David Koresh was the prophet, the messiah, and whatever he said went. There was certitude and surety for his followers, and in the end that seemed to mean more to them than his twisted doctrine. They had the answers, or so they thought. For them, most everything was in black and white.

Since Koresh's detailed interpretation of Revelation evolved over time and underwent frequent and contradictory change, it stands to reason that none of the Branch Davidians fully understood his doctrine. But that fact evidently worked to Koresh's advantage, adding to the awe felt throughout the compound. Koresh could open the seven seals. They didn't fully understand them, but what was important to them was that they thought he did.

"One has to get to heaven or the distant future to determine the truth of an effective doctrine. When some part of a doctrine is relatively simple, there is a tendency among the faithful to complicate and obscure it. Simple words are made pregnant with meaning and made to look like symbols in a secret message. There is thus an illiterate air about the most literate true believer" (*ibid.,* p. 77).

The Davidians were an intelligent lot, but they had some trouble figuring out what David Koresh was trying to tell them. With his tireless quotations, Davidian doublespeak, and endless sermons, he managed to complicate and obscure the biblical truth that Christ, not David Koresh, was their only hope of salvation.

Chapter Twenty-three

Steps and Stages of Faith

It was early morning, and infant Vernon Howell was not only awake, he wanted attention. So like every other small child his age would do in a similar circumstance, he cried for his mother. All infants have needs and cry to have them met. It seems simple enough. And the child is so young that whatever happens during those first few years will not have much effect on his or her future faith experience. Or will it?

According to John W. Fowler, a well-known researcher into the stages of spiritual faith from infancy on, "We all begin the pilgrimage of faith as infants" *(Stages of Faith,* p. 119). For we, like Vernon Howell, were highly dependent beings thrust into the world and greatly in need of our caregivers.

Although babies are born with a marvelous potential for adaptation to circumstances, if they are not held, rocked, or stimulated through communication, their ability to form loving relationships can be severely retarded, or worse yet, never activated. If physical needs such as feeding and bathing are not met in an adequate way, or if a loving person with whom a dependable relationship can be built is not present, infants' trust in the world and in themselves can be outweighed by distrust and "infantile despair" *(ibid.,* p. 120).

A sense of trust in the "primary caregiver" and the world in general is the first step—and a very important stage—in the development of a later faith in God.

In the case of Vernon Howell, it's possible that even if his young mother had been able to adequately meet all his physical needs, whatever alleged child abuse he suffered from other figures in his life during this stage may have undermined any lasting trusting relationships he may have tried to form.

As children reach the age of 7 or 8 months, they "form and retain mental images of missing objects—people and things" *(ibid.)*. When, for example, mother disappears, the baby may experience fear and panic. However, when mother reappears, the baby is "reconfirmed" in his or her sense of being and well-being. The baby's sense of trust in a dependable world thus strengthens.

During this stage of development, life plants the seeds of hope, courage, trust, and love (*ibid.,* p. 121). Or in the opposite scenario, with inconsistency and deprivation an infant's fear of abandonment may thrive. The trust developed during this phase of life will underlie all that comes later in developing a faith in God. And if fear rather than trust is the primary emotion, it may undermine all future development of faith.

Infants who do not develop the basic trust and the important personal relationships necessary at this stage may emerge as excessively self-centered or they may find themselves locked in a pattern of isolation or failed relationships *(ibid.)*.

In the case of Vernon Howell, any sense of trust that he may have developed in the dependability of the world around him was severely shaken not only by the alleged child abuse he received at a young age but also when his mother temporarily stepped out of his life when he was 2 years old.

◆◆◆

John Fowler identified another phase or stage of faith development in children when they reach the years between 2 and 7 years old. It begins with the "convergence of thought and language" *(ibid.,* p. 123).

At this point, children engage in daily experimentation, and they seek to confirm that the world consists of dependably permanent objects. Children will learn names and how to converse with their parents about what they see, hear, touch, taste, and smell.

During the second phase children daily encounter new experiences. Their thought patterns are not logical in the same sense as adult thought patterns, and so they try to make sense of their world, often filling in the "gaps" with fantasy. Children are great imitators at this time, and the examples, moods, and actions of those around them, as well as the stories told them, can profoundly affect them.

The gift "of this stage," according to Fowler, "is the birth of imagination, the ability to unify and grasp the experience-world in powerful images and as presented in stories that register the child's intuitive understandings and feelings toward the ultimate conditions of existence" *(ibid.,* p. 134).

There are dangers also, especially for children who in their religious training are subjected to vivid descriptions of hell or an overemphasis on the power of the devil.

Wrote Fowler, "This kind of faith formation—and its equivalent in other religious traditions—can ensure a dramatic 'conversion experience' by the time the child is 7 or 8" *(ibid.,* p. 132). However, Fowler went on to say that children who experience such conversions at a young age often go on to have "very rigid, brittle, and authoritarian" personalities.

"For every child whose significant others have shared religious stories, images, and symbols in ways that prove life-opening and sustaining of love, faith, and courage, there must be at least one other for whom the introduction to religion, while equally powerful, gave rise to fear, rigidity, and the brutalization of souls—both one's own and those of others," Fowler commented *(ibid.).*

During his later years, was Vernon Howell that "one other"? He certainly portrayed God as a stern, harsh, and vindictive judge.

Some well-meaning person in his childhood most probably unwittingly laid the beginnings for his view of God.

◆◆◆

During the next stage of faith development, according to Fowler, the child "begins to take on for him- or herself the stories, beliefs, and observances that symbolize belonging to his or her community. Beliefs are appropriated with literal interpretations, as are moral rules and attitudes. Symbols are taken as one-dimensional and literal in meaning" *(ibid.,* p. 149).

This is the faith stage of the school-age child, although it sometimes lingers in adolescents and adults who never progress past this point.

At this point, children learn best through stories. Now becoming better able to consider the perspective of other individuals, they develop some sort of a worldview in which they feel strong concerns about fairness and justice for all *(ibid.).*

Symbolic and dramatic materials deeply move children at this stage, "and [they] can describe in endlessly detailed narrative what has occurred" *(ibid.).*

The above attribute sounds reminiscent of Vernon Howell and his ongoing desire to discuss the Scriptures in detail with anyone willing to listen. It also helps us understand his fascination, which appears to have begun at an early age, with the book of Revelation.

Children in this stage of experience find and give meaning to their experience through story, drama, and myth *(ibid.).*

But the dangers associated with this stage concern children who rely on everything being literal and who place an excessive reliance on the concept of ultimate fairness. They may become overcontrolling and stilted perfectionists, or just the opposite—by embracing "an abasing sense of badness . . . because of mistreatment, neglect, or the apparent disfavor of significant others" *(ibid.,* p. 150).

Vernon Howell certainly took his Bible literally—too literally, one could argue. He first saw himself to have something special in common with Jesus. Having been born to an unwed mother and feeling somewhat out-of-place, he drew comfort from his sense of brotherhood, as perhaps many have before him. There would seem to be nothing wrong with this, but somewhere Vernon Howell crossed a line. Somewhere, somehow, in his mind his feelings changed from kinship to oneship, and in his mind he became the "Messiah." The vivid and dramatic prophecies of Daniel and Revelation, together with the fearsome images shown in the evangelistic series Vernon attended, fit into the fascination that persons during this stage feel with story, drama, and myth.

As for the issue of fairness, Vernon may have expected life to be fair but recognized clearly that it wasn't. Having not been born into the best of circumstances, experiencing rejection from the male figures in his life and being shuffled from home to home, he must have realized early on that his life was not like that enjoyed by many other children he knew.

The Vernon Howell described by Marc Breault and others who emerged from the cult certainly fits the mold described by Fowler for a person "stuck" at this level of spiritual maturity. At first Vernon exacted from himself an overcontrolling, stilted perfectionism. When he found that he could not meet his own standards, he enforced them upon his followers, while allowing himself what Fowler described as "an abasing sense of badness embraced because of mistreatment, neglect, or the apparent disfavor of significant others."

◆◆◆

You may be wondering what value these stages of faith have. After all, they are only characterizations or theories that most likely don't hold true in every instance.

But perhaps by dissecting the "pilgrimage of faith" that was Vernon Howell's, we may better understand how he became what he did become. And perhaps by considering these stages in the development of faith and by looking in their mirror, we may also see ourselves and be prompted to further growth in our own Christian experience.

◆◆◆

"Puberty brings with it a revolution in physical and emotional life," wrote Fowler *(ibid.,* p. 151). That revolution is often pivotal to the ongoing development of faith.

The teenage years are a time when a person's experience of the world shifts and extends beyond the family. Teenagers are influenced more than younger children not only by family but also by work, school, peers, society, the media, and perhaps, religion *(ibid.,* pp. 154, 172). In the midst of their complex and diverse range of involvement, teenagers look for some coherence to orient them and "provide a basis for identity and outlook" *(ibid.,* p. 172).

Although this "conformist stage" has its rise in adolescence, "for many adults it becomes a permanent place of equilibrium" *(ibid.).* For many teenagers and others at this level of faith, their "ultimate environment" is described in terms of interpersonal relationships. Teenagers are acutely tuned to "the expectations and judgments of . . . others" *(ibid.).* At this point in their spiritual journey, they do "not have a sure enough grasp on [their] own identity and autonomous judgment to construct and maintain an independent perspective" *(ibid.,* p. 173).

Although teenagers and others at this stage may have deep feelings over their beliefs or "ideology," they most likely have not had occasion to step outside of themselves and systematically examine their beliefs in a reflective way *(ibid.).*

One of the inherent dangers at this stage of development is the importance young people give to the expectations and evaluations of others. What others say and think of the person may be "so compellingly internalized . . . that later autonomy of judgment and action can be jeopardized." Interpersonal betrayals may lead to despair about the self, or to a "compensatory intimacy with God" *(ibid.).*

It was during Vernon Howell's teenage years that he experienced rejection by both his grandfather and by the father of the girl he wanted to marry. His "interpersonal betrayals" did, indeed, lead him to despair, and in response to that despair he did seek a "compensatory intimacy" with God. However, it's possible that by this time his lifelong feelings of rejection had been greatly internalized.

It was at this crucial point in his life, somewhere during his teenage years, that Vernon first became acquainted with the Branch Davidians. Evidently they offered him the family and acceptance that he had been longing for. They gave him a new theology that helped explain whatever rejection he felt by the Seventh-day Adventist Church. And they provided Vernon "the encounter with experiences or perspectives that lead to critical reflection on how one's beliefs and values have formed and changed" *(ibid.).* Fowler sees that "encounter" as a sign of readiness for the next stage of faith development.

◆◆◆

During the next stage of faith development, a person tends to "take seriously the burden of responsibility for his or her own commitments, lifestyle, beliefs, and attitudes" *(ibid.,* p. 182). But at the same time he or she faces certain unavoidable tensions. There is the tension between being an individual and being defined by a group or group membership. Also a natural selfishness and a selfless concern to be of service to others struggle with each other *(ibid.).*

If the person does not stop at some earlier stage, this phase normally occurs at some point during early adulthood. However, many adults, according to Fowler, do not reach it until they are 30 or 40. During this stage the individual differentiates his or her personal outlook from that of others. Persons on this level tend to engage in critical reflection on their identities and outlooks.

One of the dangers facing this stage, according to Fowler, is an excessive confidence in the ability of the person to think and reason things through for himself or herself. Sometimes a sort of egotism develops in which the person overabsorbs "reality" and the perspectives of others into his or her own world view *(ibid.,* pp. 182, 183).

Persons at this stage of faith find themselves disillusioned with their compromises and recognize that life is more complex than they originally thought. In response they press on toward a more multileveled approach to the truths in their life *(ibid.).*

It seemed that Vernon Howell always took seriously "the burden of responsibility for his . . . own commitments, lifestyle, beliefs, and attitudes" *(ibid.,* p. 182). During his return to the Tyler church in Texas, he felt the tension between being an individual and having his moral behavior defined by the standards of the Seventh-day Adventist Church.

Later as a new convert to the Branch Davidian way of thinking, Howell once more found himself challenged in terms of his behavior. Branch Davidians, were, for the most part, a conservative, strict-living lot. It seems that Vernon rejected the values not only of the Seventh-day Adventist Church but also of the Branch Davidians. The struggle within him between the "natural selfishness and the selfless concern to be of service to others" was won by his selfish nature. Vernon expected his followers to live the selfless life, but he rejected it for himself and shaped his theology and that of the Davidians who followed him to fit his own personal moral standards (or lack of them).

Vernon certainly seemed to fit the description of Fowler in terms of the "excessive confidence" in his own theories. A sort of egotism, that his was the one and only right way, was one of the hallmarks of his own worldview.

Howell may have been disillusioned with the moral compromises he had made earlier in his life and came to realize that life was more complex than he had originally thought. In response he constructed his own detailed "multileveled" approach to the truths in his life. The approach he took just happened to do away with many of the values that he had been taught, and it allowed him to do whatever pleased him.

◆◆◆

Fowler goes on to describe two more—and higher—levels of faith. He defines faith and belief separately. (Fowler here speaks of faith as it stands alone—the exact set of beliefs a person developed faith in is not the primary purpose of his discussion.) The top level of faith that he described is "the culminating image of mature faith."

Those who reach this final dimension of faith have not reached perfection, according to Fowler, but they do "shake our usual criteria of normalcy. Their heedlessness to self-preservation and the vividness of their taste and feel for transcendent moral and religious actuality give their actions and words an extraordinary and often unpredictable quality" *(ibid.,* p. 200).

Such persons live "with felt participation in a power that unifies and transforms the world" *(ibid.,* p. 201).

Fowler cautions against ascribing this type of faith to a Jim Jones or an Ayatollah Khomeini. The highest level of faith development as, defined him, includes an "inclusiveness of community . . . [and] radical commitment to justice and love and of selfless passion for a transformed world, a world made over not in *their* images, but in accordance with an intentionality both divine and transcendent" *(ibid.).*

Those who exhibit this type of faith are rare—very rare, he believes.

◆◆◆

In addition to Fowler's research into the stages of faith, it might be of interest to consider Valuegenesis, "a study of the influence of family, church, and school on the faith, values, and commitment of Adventist youth." The Valuegenesis study assessed "faith maturity" among Adventist youth using an index developed by the Search Institute for its national study of Protestant youth and adults.

"As measured in this index, faith maturity is a process, not a product. It is much more than a set of right beliefs, it is a way of life. It is reflected in the priorities, dispositions, and behaviors of people."

In this respect, faith maturity sounds similar to the highest level of faith described by Fowler. Those with a mature faith allow that faith to influence their actions and transform their life.

The Valuegenesis report describes three factors that affect the maturity of faith shown by young adults. They are: the family, the church congregation, and the school.

Research conducted in the preparation of this report found that when home, school, and church influences were all ineffective, only 7 percent of high school seniors would exhibit both high faith maturity and high loyalty to the Seventh-day Adventist denomination.

When one of the primary influences was effective—for example, the child had an ineffective home and church experience, but the school she or he attended was excellent—the percentage of high school seniors who exhibited both high faith maturity and high loyalty to the Seventh-day Adventist denomination rose to 17 percent.

When two of the three factors were effective, 30 percent of the high school seniors revealed high faith maturity and high denominational loyalty.

And when students had a strong Christian home life, a caring church, and an effective school experience, 53 percent of them displayed both high faith maturity and high loyalty to the Seventh-day Adventist Church in their senior year of high school.

◆◆◆

In the case of Vernon Howell, we might draw several conclusions after considering this information. First of all, even if his home life was less than what might be considered the ideal, the probability of his developing a level of high faith maturity and denominational loyalty could have increased with a highly effective experience at either church or school. However, even if he had had a strong and positive family background and had "effective" experiences both at the church and school, he still could have been one of the 47 percent who did not exhibit high faith maturity or denominational loyalty even after being raised in what would appear to be the most conducive circumstances. Ultimately, there is a matter of personal choice involved.

Also, we must note that there were three factors affecting the emergence of faith maturity and denominational loyalty. It is all too easy to point to Vernon's childhood and say, "Unwed teenage mother, broken home, alleged abuse, rejection by father figures—what could we have done?"

There is always room for reflection on what the Seventh-day Adventist Church could have done that might have altered the sad ending to this story. Some of the painful questions that we must raise are Where were we for Bonnie Clark when she was an unwed teenage mother? Were we as concerned as we should have been? Was there something that could have been done for her in terms of support (or for Vernon at a later age) that might have altered the course of his life?

We cannot undo whatever mistakes may have been made, but we can all examine ourselves to see what we might do in the future.

The Valuegenesis study, in addition to describing the role that family, church, and school play in the development of faith in our children, also suggested that of the 41 elements influencing the effectiveness of home, church, and school, three stood out as directly strengthening faith and loyalty. They are: the quality of family worship; a thinking climate and caring, supportive leaders in the church congregation; and the quality of the church school program.

It seems worthy of note that the "thinking climate," something we have seen in this book as of crucial importance for avoiding involvement in cult-type organizations, is one of the most dynamic factors seen in the development of faith. This affirms the idea that we must teach children and youth to think for themselves.

"The education that consists in the training of the memory, tending to discourage independent thought, has a moral bearing which is too little appreciated. As the student sacrifices the power to reason and judge for himself, he becomes incapable of discriminating between truth and error and falls an easy prey to deception. He is easily led to follow tradition and custom" *(Education,* p. 230).

Ellen White also encouraged manual or vocational training as a means of encouraging young people to think for themselves. "Practical work encourages close observation and independent thought. Rightly performed, it tends to develop that practical wisdom which we call common sense. It develops ability to plan and execute, strengthens courage and perseverance, and calls for the exercise of tact and skill" *(ibid.,* p. 220).

Perhaps as the church considers how Adventist schools can better prepare young people to be independent thinkers, it should place more emphasis on mixing manual labor with studies.

◆◆◆

When it comes to faith maturity, it might be true that the only certain thing is that nothing is certain.

We can be sure that there are stages of faith, because the Bible talks about "growing up into Christ," and there are certainly stages of growth and development. We've all experienced them.

Furthermore, before John Fowler ever wrote his book about stages of faith, Ellen White wrote: "Those who are thus connected with Christ learn constantly of Him, passing through the successive stages of progress in Christian experience" *(The Upward Look,* p. 235).

"Those who halt in the Christian life, and make no advance beyond the first stages of religion, do not realize the necessity of becoming partakers of the divine nature, to push the triumphs of the cross" *(Words to the Young,* p. 7).

"If [people] ask in faith, they will increase in knowledge and ability. If they depend upon God day by day, the stages of development will show a symmetrical growth heavenward" *(The Ellen G. White 1888 Materials,* p. 1820).

Speculation as to what "stage of faith" Vernon Howell and his partners-in-siege possibly attained might serve no useful purpose other than shedding some light on why they did what they did. And an evaluation of the level of faith development attained by Adventist youth might also be useless unless it results in some personal action by those who choose to learn from it.

It seems that both Fowler's conclusions and the findings of the Valuegenesis study confirm the importance of the home in the development of faith in young people. Both also point to the church and school as important factors.

Also it appears that God is calling Seventh-day Adventists to the highest type of faith—that life-changing and sometimes gut-wrenching commitment that people just won't make without understanding the rationale behind it. High moral standards in a secular world are not easy to uphold. And those who have not reflected on their meaning, building a firm biblical foundation for their faith, might opt for a different doctrine.

If John Fowler is right when he insists that the highest "stage of faith" is exceedingly rare, one would have to consider that it might also be rare among Seventh-day Adventists. A somewhat disturbing thought, if you happen to believe that a high level of faith maturity will be necessary to withstand whatever tests and trauma just might be waiting around the corner for Bible-believing Seventh-day Adventists.

If Vernon Howell, through the events at Ranch Apocalypse, has shaken us to the extent that we all go back to reexamine the foundations of our faith, he just might have done us at least one favor after all.

Chapter Twenty-four

Escaping the Extremes

What could I have done differently? is the question in the minds and hearts of distraught parents, friends, and relatives of those who died at Ranch Apocalypse.

Still another question haunts us: How can we avoid another Waco-type episode?

Answers do not come easily, and for some questions there seem to be no answers at all. Seductive leaders are nothing new. If Lucifer could entice one third of the angels from Paradise with the promise of something better, it should come as no surprise that other leadership types have been able to repeat his successes on an earthly scale. After all, it seems that humans should have much more to be dissatisfied with than angels enjoying a blissful existence in heaven. Yet the angels, like all of us today, seemed to have been drawn to the idea of something better.

◆◆◆

Something better. That was what Vernon Howell/David Koresh told Seventh-day Adventist young people he could offer them. A deeper experience, an addition to, not a denial of, what they already believed.

According to Pastor Phil Payne, David Koresh often began his recruitment solicitations to Seventh-day Adventists by asking them, "Are you living up to everything you know you should do?" with specific referral to the writings of Ellen White. Since few—if any—Adventists may actually keep her injunctions to the letter, the answer would usually be no, followed by some comment about wishing for a deeper experience.

Koresh would then follow up by offering them something concrete, something he described as better, something they would be willing to die for.

Bruce Manners, in an editorial for the South Pacific Division *Record,* suggested that assurance of salvation is one area in which Adventists have been hesitant to speak. Some Adventists take statements from Ellen White warning against the once-saved-always-saved attitude and carry them to the opposite extreme.

But because they are not sure of their own salvation, they are vulnerable to the suggestions of someone like David Koresh, who promises to give them that assurance.

"Individuals who know they are accepted by God will be less inclined to go searching for something extra," wrote Manners. "We need to emphasize that we can have the assurance of salvation now. There are no doubts about our salvation when we are in Christ. And as long as we remain in Christ we have salvation."

◆◆◆

Biblical knowledge by itself is another safeguard against recruitment by cultish organizations. Ellen White warned Seventh-day Adventists that fanaticism would again be a threat during the last days of earth's history and that they must study the Scriptures to learn how to avoid falling into extremism.

"Let the people of God arouse out of sleep and begin in earnest the work of repentance and reformation; let them search the Scriptures to learn the truth as it is in Jesus; let them make an entire consecration to God, and evidence will not be wanting that Satan is still active and vigilant. With all possible deception he will manifest his power, calling to his aid all the fallen angels of his realm" *(The Great Controversy,* p. 398).

"As the end draws near, the enemy will work with all his power to bring in fanaticism among us. He would rejoice to see Seventh-day Adventists going to such extremes that they would be branded by the world as a body of fanatics. Against this danger I am bidden to warn ministers and lay members. Our work is to teach men and women to build on a true foundation, to plant their feet on a plain 'Thus saith the Lord'" *(Gospel Workers,* p. 316).

Perhaps the following quotation from Ellen White helps explain why, despite intense efforts by church members in some areas, the doctrines of David Koresh still spread: "Fanaticism, once started and left unchecked, is as hard to quench as a fire which has obtained hold of a building" *(Selected Messages,* book 2, p. 35).

Seventh-day Adventism began with intense Bible study, and that study is just as necessary today as it was throughout its previous history.

"We are fast entering the perils of the last days, when views which conflict with the Word of God will be presented by men of giant intellects, and we ought to be able to show the falsity of their claims. Our children also should be thoroughly furnished with Bible truth, so that they will not be moved by every new doctrine presented in their hearing" *(Signs of the Times,* Mar. 6, 1879).

◆◆◆

Although we must study our Bibles to understand God's will for our lives and to avoid dangerous movements such as the one at Ranch Apocalypse, Bible study in and of itself might not be enough. After all, David Koresh knew his Bible extremely well, which made him all the more dangerous. He would claim that Scripture supported all his doctrines. Koresh exhibited an uncanny ability to pull texts from here, there, and yonder in defense of whatever point he was trying to make. And therein lay the problem—his method of interpretation.

The Davidians found all kinds of meanings and interpretations in the Bible that most Seventh-day Adventists have never seen. Davidians believed that predictions of the ATF raid, a divine slaughter of Seventh-day Adventists, and David Koresh as the sinful messiah all had solid scriptural support. How could persons who studied the Bible so much have gotten such strange messages from its pages?

Perhaps they lost sight of Christ in their quest for biblical truth, because in order to know the Bible's teachings, we need to know personally the One the Bible is all about. We can't follow Jesus without knowing His Word for ourselves, nor can we really know the Word unless we are exclusively followers of Jesus.

"There is one great central truth to be kept ever before the mind in the searching of the Scriptures," wrote Ellen White. "Christ and Him crucified. Every other truth is invested with influence and power corresponding to its relation to this theme. It is only in the light of the cross that we can discern the exalted character of the law of God" *(The SDA Bible Commentary,* Ellen G. White Comments, vol. 6, p. 1084).

In addition to the above possibility, Seventh-day Adventists would argue that the whole Davidian system of Bible interpretation is wrong.

The Davidians took many of the prophecies given to Old Testament prophets and applied them to their movement. Many of these prophecies were made to the nation of Israel and were conditional upon ancient Israel's faithfulness to God.

The Bible states that if the children of Israel had followed God's plan, they would have manifested holiness of character and enjoyed the blessings of health. They would have had a superior intellect, thanks to the lasting effects of a healthy lifestyle, that would have been handed down from generation to generation. In addition, they would have had extraordinary skill in agriculture, animal husbandry, and craftsmanship. All this would have led to the prophesied unparalleled prosperity and national greatness. (See *The SDA Bible Commentary,* vol. 4, pp. 27, 28.)

According to God's plan, other nations would have noticed Israel's national greatness, and they in turn would either choose to follow the successful example of the Israelites or eventually be uprooted by the spread of the Israelite nation.

"The glorious era of David and Solomon marked what might have been the beginning of Israel's golden age" *(ibid.,* p. 31). The queen of Sheba, upon her visit to see Solomon's greatness, remarked, "The half was not told me" (1 Kings 10:7).

Tragically, Israel experienced a speedy decline after that great era because of their unfaithfulness to God. Although He had to punish them with captivity and numerous adversities throughout the years, God still continued to give them prophetic guidance.

The Seventh-day Adventist Bible Commentary, volume 4, pages 25-38, offers a detailed and biblically documented discussion of Israel's trials and tribulations before the time of Christ.

Israel's "unwillingness to submit to the restrictions and requirements of God prevented them, to a great extent, from reaching the high standard which He desired them to attain, and from receiving the blessing which He was ready to bestow upon them" *(Patriarchs and Prophets,* p. 378).

God worked long with the nation, but when the Messiah finally came, they "received him not" (John 1:11). They had "overlooked those scriptures that point to the humiliation of Christ's first Advent, and misapplied those that speak of the glory of His second coming" *(The Desire of Ages,* p. 30).

Seventh-day Adventists see in the Bible a spiritual Israel, God's church, replacing the literal Israel. Because many of the prophecies to literal Israel were conditional upon their obedience to God, and because the conditions were never met, some of those prophecies may never be fulfilled (see *The SDA Bible Commentary,* vol. 4, p. 34).

But David Koresh and the Branch Davidians took many of those Old Testament prophecies and applied them, in whatever manner they chose, to events happening in their personal lives.

Again this is foreign to the method of Bible interpretation that

Seventh-day Adventists have relied on. Seventh-day Adventists take the Bible as a whole—in its historical, cultural, and literary context—in order to arrive at its true meaning.

Koresh took isolated verses and applied them to himself—for example, the passage in the Song of Solomon that spoke of numerous wives and concubines.

When claiming to be the lamb of Revelation, but different than the biblical Christ, Koresh seems to have ignored numerous Old Testament references to the sacrificial lamb, which pointed forward to the Christ of the Bible as being the antitypical lamb. And when he presented himself as the sinful messiah, and eventually Christ Himself, Koresh seemed to forget the numerous references in the Bible to God's abhorrence of sin, as well as His acceptance of Christ's sacrifice as a complete atonement for that sin.

Because of his photographic memory, Koresh could outquote almost anyone in both Scripture and the writings of Ellen White. Caught up in a torrent of misapplied texts, his followers evidently did not see that he used them totally out of context and out of harmony with a logical manner of biblical interpretation.

If you were to interpret any ancient book, it seems logical that in order to learn its true meaning you would want not only to read the entire book, but also to understand its historical setting. Seventh-day Adventist beliefs are biblically based on the entire Scriptures. The Old Testament, with its prophecies pointing toward the time of Christ, helps clarify the New Testament, and vice versa.

Perhaps we individual Seventh-day Adventists need to rebuild the foundations of our faith, from the ground up, and confirm for ourselves its truths. "There are some in the church who need to cling to the pillars of our faith, to settle down and find rock bottom, instead of drifting on the surface of excitement, and moving from impulse" (*Testimonies,* vol. 4, p. 74).

"I would say to my brethren and sisters, Keep close to the instruction found in the Word of God. Dwell upon the rich truths of the Scriptures. Thus only can you become one in Christ" *(Selected Messages,* book 1, p. 171).

◆◆◆

For those who desire it, salvation is available. But as Lonnie Little wishes, all of us should remember: "We are saved by grace."

Each of us will be buffeted by powerful, persuasive elements as we near the end of time. As we remember Waco individually and as a church, may we resolve to press together, anchor our faith in the Bible, and receive the power that is available only through a personal relationship with Jesus Christ. With this—and only with this—we can be safe.

In the beautiful words of Jesus, an invitation is open to us all: "Come unto me, all ye that labour and are heavy laden, and I will give you rest" (Matt. 11:28).

With the invitation comes also an assurance: "My sheep hear my voice. I know them, and they follow me. I give them eternal life, and they will never perish. No one will snatch them out of my hand" (John 10:27, 28, NRSV).

Epilogue

Perhaps it would be too easy to neatly wrap up our assumptions about Waco and reach "final" conclusions. After all, we are talking about people's lives here. And the tragic incident involved complex sociological, psychological, and religious issues.

You may not have agreed with everything you read in this book . . . and that might be good. Its purpose was not so much to answer questions as to inspire thought.

In harmony with that goal, we would like to leave you with some of the questions posed throughout this book, questions that we all might do well to think about.

• Should we blame what happened at Waco on David Koresh's childhood, or did the congregations and schools he attended somehow fail him also? And what role did personal choice play for him and his followers?

• What impact does rock music and its softer forms have on our church? Since numerous rock musicians have not formed cults or staged shoot-outs with the federal government, is it fair to include music as an influential and damaging factor in the life of David Koresh?

• What role might the typical Texan's attitude toward weaponry have had in Koresh's life? What might be the effects of violent hunting videos or war play in childhood? How did the peaceful and pacifist Branch Davidians suddenly start wielding machine guns and tossing grenades?

• What will *you* do if ever confronted with someone trying to exercise mind control over you? Will you recognize it before it is too late? Were the Branch Davidians morally responsible for their actions, or were they under some sort of deluded and helpless spell, or both?

• What can your local congregation do if someone like David Koresh starts recruiting your young people? Should there be a renewed vigilance on our part against this type of movement? How far can we go without jeopardizing the liberty of church members?

• Have we, in interpreting Ellen White, followed the same principles of taking her writings as a whole and in their context that we hold so valuable in interpreting Scripture?

• What role can diet play in keeping our minds clear to detect error? What about physical or manual labor? Are we doing well in these areas to help young people develop balanced minds?

• Have we studied for ourselves the biblical foundation of the Adventist message, or have we merely accepted the explanations of someone else?

• If you saw your child or a dear friend under the influence of mind control, what would you do?

• Does the church do all it could or should for young unwed mothers, such as Bonnie Haldeman? Are there persons willing to show God's love and encouragement to children who feel rejection?

• What other lessons should we learn in the wake of Waco?

◆◆◆

The next chapter in this book may be written by you!